LAKE DISTRICT

▲ Ashness Bridge and Skiddaw

Produced jointly by the Publishing Division of
The Automobile Association and the Ordnance Survey

Editorial contributors: Harry Griffin (Traditional Sports); Dr William Rollinson (Man in the Landscape); Ronald Sands (Literary Lakeland); Rebecca Snelling (Fact File); Andrew and Isabel Wilson (A to Z Gazetteer); John Wyatt (Lakeland Wildlife, Fell Walking, Gazetteer revisions to new edition, Tours and Walks in the Lake District).

Original photography: Sarah King and World Photography

Typeset by Microset Graphics Ltd., Basingstoke, Hampshire
Colour separation by BTB Colour Reproduction Ltd., Whitchurch, Hampshire
Printed and bound by William Clowes Limited, Beccles and London

Maps extracted from the Ordnance Survey's 1:63,360 Tourist Series, 1:25,000 Pathfinder Series and 1:250,000 Routemaster Series with the permission of Her Majesty's Stationery Office. Crown copyright.

Additions to the maps by the Cartographic Department of The Automobile Association and the Ordnance Survey.

Produced by the Publishing Division of The Automobile Association.

Distributed in the United Kingdom by the Ordnance Survey, Southampton, and the Publishing Division of The Automobile Association, Fanum House, Basingstoke, Hampshire RG21 2EA.

First edition 1984
Reprinted 1984, 1986, 1987, 1988, 1989, 1990
Revised edition 1992

A CIP catalogue record of this book is available from the British Library.

AA ISBN 0 7495 0373 4 (hardback)
AA ISBN 0 7495 0383 1 (softback)
OS ISBN 0 319 00285 3 (hardback)
OS ISBN 0 319 00276 4 (softback)

Published by The Automobile Association and the Ordnance Survey.

Introduction: Tarn Hows from Sawrey viewpoint

Contents

▲ River Caldbeck, Caldbeck village

Introduction

The Lake District has spellbound the adventurous
traveller since the earliest days of tourism two
hundred years ago. Thousands of people escape to the
freedom and beauty of the dales and fells each year.
Whatever the weather, at any time of the year, the
Lake District exerts a special fascination. Whether you
are in search of the solitude Wordsworth treasured, or
bustling market towns, this guide will provide the key.
It explores the history, traditions and wildlife, and
describes the towns, villages and hamlets of the Lake
District. Walks and motor tours seek out the hidden
corners and the finest scenery.
Written entirely by people who live and work in the
Lake District, backed by the AA's research expertise
and the Ordnance Survey's mapping, this guide is
equally useful to the faithful who return to the Lakes
year after year and to the first-time visitor.

Man in the Landscape

For many people, the fells of the Lake District represent the epitome of the 'natural' landscape – the eternal hills, the wild, cloud-catching mountain summits, the lonely, barren upland tarns, the brawling, racing, tumbling becks, the silent, sombre forests – a seemingly timeless, unchanging landscape, fundamentally the same today as it was 4–5,000 years ago. Yet nothing could be further from the truth, for the present landscape of the Lake District is essentially 'man-made', the product of the interaction of Man with his environment, and everywhere it is possible to see evidence of the way in which Man has moulded and modified his environment over the centuries rather as if an artist has used, re-used, and re-used again a single canvas – look carefully and it is often possible to detect the outlines of an earlier picture.

Without the presence of Man, the landscape would look entirely different from the one we know; mixed oak forest would colonise the lower fells and above that, to a height of about 2,000 ft, pine and birch woodland would blanket the upper fells so that only the highest mountain peaks projected above the forest cover. It is difficult to appreciate that familiar and much-loved summits such as Cat Bells, Wansfell Pike, and Helm Crag were once submerged in a sea of green forest. Similarly, without Man, the valleys of Great Langdale, Borrowdale, Wasdale Head and Newlands would be choked with sedges and alder swamp; indeed, it takes all the power of imagination to conjure up such a scene for this is not the landscape which is known and cherished by millions of people today. So when did the transformation begin? The answer, quite simply, is about 5,000 years ago when, for the first time, Man met the challenge of the environment and began to control it – almost imperceptibly at first, but with an inexorability which ultimately led to the present landscape.

Stone axe factories
Although Mesolithic family groups, the first nomadic hunting and collecting communities, had inhabited the coastal areas since about 5,500 BC, they made little impact on the environment for they were largely governed by it. However, the next groups to arrive in the area, Neolithic peoples, were far more ambitious; as well as developing the arts of crop-growing and the domestication of animals, they made a positive response to the ecological challenge of the forest by the mass production of sharp, polished, hafted stone axes which could effectively clear large areas for crops and animals. Moreover, the Neolithic Cumbrians were skilled field geologists; they were clearly aware that only certain types of fine-grained volcanic rocks would produce the sharpest axes. Therefore they actively sought these outcrops and the evidence of 'factory workings' has been found on the Langdale Pikes and the Scafells as well as on other fellsides. Here axes were roughly chipped out before being carried along forest tracks to the coast where they were finely sharpened and honed using the sharp quartz sand of the sea-shore. When they were hafted in a wooden handle Man possessed a tool with which he could shape his destiny, for in some respects the development of the polished stone axe marks one of the revolutions in human history as great as the Industrial Revolution of the 19th century and the Social Revolution of our own day.

But it was not merely the stone axe which began the process of modification of the landscape; the domestication of animals meant that sheep, pigs, goats and cattle ranged widely in the newly-created clearings, grubbing, nibbling and browsing any new green shoots and therefore reducing the rate of natural regeneration of the forest cover, a process which continued almost unhindered until the re-afforestation of the 18th, 19th and 20th centuries.

Stone circles
If the felling of the primeval forest was an early expression of Man's impact on his environment, then the building in the early Bronze Age of the huge stone circles is arguably more tangible. Demanding, as they did, a high degree of social cooperation, they also mark a significant change in Man's awareness of himself, for now for the first time he was building something which would outlast his own life-span. The arguments about their purpose continue to rage – religious centres, market places, prehistoric computers – perhaps we will never know, but these massive stone monuments seldom fail to exert a fascination for the visitor. The largest is Long Meg and her

Castlerigg, near Keswick, a prehistoric henge monument in a superb setting. The functions of this, and similar structures, may never be clearly understood

Hardknott Fort – built by the Romans to command the whole of Eskdale

Daughters near Salkeld, but the best known and most visited is at Castlerigg near Keswick.

Few Bronze Age settlement sites have so far been identified, though the characteristic burial cairns dot the landscape. From about 500 BC the technology of the Iron Age accelerated the process of forest clearance, and settlements penetrated many of the inner valleys of the central fells, and in particular concentrated on the limestones which surround the uplands. Here, the distinctive enclosing walls within which are animal pens and the foundations of circular huts, can be seen in such locations as Ewe Close, near Crosby Ravensworth, High Borrans, near Windermere, Aughertree, near Ireby, and in the Kentmere valley. But the Iron Age marks a more sinister landscape development – the construction of hill forts; the largest is on the summit of Carrock Fell (2,174ft) dominating Mungrisdale, but more spectacular are those on Castle Crag, Borrowdale, and Castle Crag, overlooking Haweswater. Whether or not such fortifications were constructed as a response to inter-tribal strife or the fear of Roman invasion is unknown.

The Romans

It has been said that the Lake District was almost at vanishing point on the scale of Romanisation and, indeed, the civilising effect of Rome was minimal, but the impact of military might on the landscape is very apparent. Arriving in the fells at the end of the first century AD, the Romans subjugated the troublesome native Brigantes by a method as ingenious as it was effective; from a fort at Watercrook near Kendal, they drove a road through the high fells over Wrynose and Hardknott passes, to the sea at Ravenglass, thereby neatly dividing and dominating the native heartland. Along this road, like beads on a string, cohort forts, housing 500 men, were established. At Waterhead, near Ambleside, the remains of the fort with its turrets, granary, HQ, and commandant's house, can still be traced, but to savour to the full the power of Rome, a visit should be made to Hardknott Fort, perched eyrie-like above the Esk valley, commanding unsurpassed views of Eskdale and the Scafells. Here it requires but little imagination to reconstruct the stone-

built granary and headquarters, the bath-house outside the walls and the wooden barrack blocks once inhabited by troops from Dalmatia, modern Yugoslavia. From Hardknott the military road ran along Eskdale to Ravenglass; sadly the fort there was largely destroyed by the railway in 1850, but the bath-house remains; known as Walls Castle, it is one of the most complete, upstanding Roman buildings in the north of England.

Probably the most spectacular of all the Roman roads in Lakeland is that which crosses the 2,000ft summit of High Street. Although intended only for foot soldiers, it probably connected the fort at Waterhead with the one at Brougham near Penrith and even today, suitably shod fell-walkers can literally follow in the steps of the Romans.

The Dark Ages

Roman rule in the Lake District seems to have ended in the late 4th century and from then until the 7th century the so-called Dark Ages are centuries of uncertainty, peopled by the *Cymry*, the Celtic descendants of the Brigantes, and by shadowy, legendary figures such as Urien, Vortigern, and Arthur. Although several Celtic river and mountain names still exist, the impact of the Celts on the landscape remains unclear. In the 7th century, however, people of Anglian farming stock moved from Northumbria into the Eden valley, the Cumbrian coastal plain and Furness and Cartmel, seeking the best and most fertile soils. Their settlements can be identified today by place-name elements such as *-ton, -ham,* and *-ington,* but in addition these Anglian farmers have left beautiful carved stone crosses; the finest in the north of England is at Bewcastle in northern Cumbria, but there are splendid examples at Irton, Dacre, Kendal, and Urswick.

The Norse settlers

If the Anglian settlers farmed the good quality lands surrounding the uplands, then the Viking peoples who followed them in the 9th and 10th centuries sought out an environment with which they and their ancestors were familiar – the fells and dales. Often synonymous with looting, rape, and pillage, the Vikings have had a bad press, mainly because their history was written by their enemies, but here in the Lake District the story is different. The Scandinavians who settled here were not the stereotyped horned-helmeted warriors of the sagas – they were, in fact, peaceful third or fourth generation Vikings who came not directly from the *viks* of Norway, but from Ireland and the Isle of Man. Nevertheless, they brought with them a characteristic settlement pattern of valley farms and summer pastures, or *saeters,* at the head of the valley or on the fellsides. That their ancestors came from western Norway rather than Denmark is revealed by place-name elements such as *-fell, -booth, -gill, -slack,* and *-beck* and the most common of all, *-thwaite.* The present map bristles with *-thwaites* which, significantly, means a clearing, usually in the forest, and the concentration is most marked within the uplands.

As well as place-names and, indeed, thousands of dialect words, the Scandinavians, like the Anglians, left carved stone crosses. Erected at a time when the Vikings were nominally Christian, many of the crosses bear a fusion of Christian and pagan symbols. Such crosses can be seen at Muncaster, Penrith, Kirkby Stephen, Brigham, but the finest of all is at Gosforth, near the coast,

St Bees – the intricate doorway of the Norman monastery church. This is the finest decoration of its kind in Cumbria. There is further Norman work inside the church

where a slender sandstone column tells the story of Ragnarok and the crucifixion.

Behind Fell Foot Farm in Little Langdale is a terraced mound bearing remarkable similarities to Tynwald Hill in the Isle of Man. Many authorities interpret this as a 'thingmount' or Norse parliament field. If they are correct, this is a unique monument to the Viking age in Lakeland.

The Normans

For most of England, 1066 meant the Norman conquest – but not for the Lake District, which remained under Scottish domination until 1092 when William II captured Carlisle and settled the region with his Norman followers. The Normans, of course, feared for their souls and consequently gave grants of land to the Church to ensure immortality; almost all the major Cumbrian monasteries were founded in the 12th century – Wetheral, Carlisle, Lanercost, St Bees, Furness, Holm Cultram – and although they were on the periphery of the Lake District, most owned land within the fells, many created granges or home farms, as well as clearing the waste and creating huge sheep-runs. None was more diligent in this process of land development than the great Cistercian abbey of Furness; already possessing much of the Furness peninsula, by the 13th century the abbey had acquired thousands of acres of fell land including all the area between Coniston Water and Windermere, part of Borrowdale (Fountains Abbey owned the other half), and upper Eskdale.

Scottish raids

But all was not sweetness and light; the 14th century was a period of fierce border warfare and, following the battle of Bannockburn, the Lake District soon felt the scourge of the Scots. Penrith, Appleby, and Carlisle were repeatedly besieged and destroyed, in 1316 Copeland and Furness were attacked, and in 1322 Robert Bruce again raided Furness, crossed the sands of Morecambe Bay and devastated Lancaster. The response was

Above and right: Lakeland views. Both show the impact of man's hand on the landscape. Even mighty Scafell (above) has drystone walls marching across it. The majority of such walls were built in the 18th and 19th centuries, when the fells were being enclosed

Townend, Troutbeck – one of the best examples of a 17th-century stone-built farmhouse

predictable; scores of stoutly-built pele towers were constructed as a defence against further raids. Several, such as Sizergh, Hutton and Muncaster became part of stately homes, while others such as Kentmere and Wraysholme became farm outbuildings; their presence in the landscape a constant reminder of border conflict.

The dissolution of the monasteries – 'the Great Northern Tragedy' – undoubtedly had an effect on the landscape, yet sheep continued to be tended, the charcoal-burner still worked his pitsteads, and the woodland was depleted for fuel and for ships. Around Kendal, Hawkshead and Ambleside the woollen cloth industry flourished, while at the end of the 16th century, the Company of the Mines Royal, a Crown monopoly, began to open silver, lead and, later, copper mines.

The winds of change

In the late 17th and early 18th centuries the winds of change swept through Cumbria. This was the period, rather later than in other areas of England, when the old timber-framed farmhouses were demolished and built again in stone; although there are earlier examples, most of the dated lintel stones fall between 1640 and 1750, indicating 'the Great Rebuilding in Stone'.

From 1750 until about 1850 there occurred one of the last great major landscape changes – the enclosure of the open fells into a stone network of fields and intakes. During the Napoleonic Wars when the price of food was high, it paid the farmers to improve and reclaim the fellsides and gangs of itinerant craftsmen enmeshed the hills with a web of drystone walls.

The 18th century brought the turnpike roads and the early tourists in search of the mock perils of the 'picturesque'; the 19th century brought the railways and the *nouveax riches* settlers to the shores of Windermere, able to travel to Manchester for a day's work in the Cotton Exchange but enjoy a late evening meal overlooking the placid surface of Windermere. In the 20th century the pressures on the landscape have increased a hundredfold; the need for great forestry estates, the demand for reservoirs to supply distant towns and cities with water, the expansion of great slate-quarries on the hillsides, the pressure of tourism which often destroys what it seeks to enjoy; the erosion of footpaths by sheer weight of numbers, the 'second home syndrome' – yet despite all that the Lake District remains a unique place, a landscape made by Man but no less beautiful for that. Long may it remain what Wordsworth envisaged:

> . . . a sort of national property, in which every man has a right and an interest who has an eye to perceive and a heart to enjoy.

Lakeland Wildlife

Seen from an aeroplane, the Lake District's complicated landscape is much fretted, pierced, buckled and scored, with a jagged jumble of crags and ridges, and a shining labyrinth of lakes and watercourses. It is as if stupendous forces had plucked and folded and crushed the land together to compress much into little. And so they did. In that great crushing of the earth millions of years ago there was unimaginable heat, rocks melted and burst, were slaked by the sea, smothered in dust storms and sculpted by deluge and ice. All these forces eventually created the Lake District landforms that we know today. There are three principal scenic types – in the north the angular landscape formed from shales of the ancient sedimentary Skiddaw Slates; in the centre the craggy heights of the Borrowdale Volcanic series; and in the south the softer tree-clad landscape of the Silurian Slates. Within these large themes are many intricate details, and each detail is inhabited by a complex tangle of wildlife.

The scourge of the axe
When Mesolithic man settled on the west coast of the Lake District some 6,000 years ago the forest stretched as far as the eye could see. High on some fells where soil has become exposed by erosion, it is still possible today to recover fragments of birch and pine root remaining from that ancient forest, for the tree cover reached the highest peaks. On the same fells it is possible to find one of the first causes of the forest's undoing, for at several places where a certain very hard rock occurs on the surface, you can walk on the chipping floors of

stone-age man's axe factories. When polished and sharpened these prehistoric stone axes were very efficient tools.

For 4,000 years men hacked away at the forest cover, clearing even larger areas. Domestic animals like cattle and sheep prevented any natural regeneration by eating seedling trees. The result is a landscape largely cloaked in grass and short herbage. Is there any of the old forest left? Most naturalists would say not, though there is a possibility that the Keskadale woods in Newlands valley are a remnant of the primeval oak wood.

Lower down the fell sides a remarkable feature of the Lake District is the juniper scrubland. Juniper is our only native cypress. The berries were once valuable in medicine but are now mainly used for flavouring gin. Juniper charcoal was the best, and was much favoured by local mills making gunpowder. What is fascinating is the enormous variety of shapes the shrubs assume: some as flat as plates, some with tall spires, some twisted like bonsais. In similar situations, but on the crags, is often a profusion of bilberry, offering a rare feast of fruit if the birds don't get there first. Heather and ling favour the deeper soils of the Skiddaw Slate and Silurians.

Using the woodlands
It is the valley broadleaved woodlands of the southern Silurian soils, the northern Skiddaw Slates, and the perimeter limestones that are the richest habitats for wildlife. Through history these woodlands made an important contribution to the economy of the Lake District. For centuries they

were harvested and coppiced. An example of the prosperity which such woodlands could bring, and of the variety of uses to which they could be put, can be found in the records of Furness Abbey. Cutting rights were let here, and rights to feed swine on the acorns. Bark was sold for tanning. Charcoal was made, as were cartwheels, cups, dishes, and barrels.

Coppice wood was cut every 12–15 years in each wood. Its all-important use was to make charcoal, increasingly so as new sources of iron ore were found in the district, since charcoal was an essential ingredient of the smelting process until coal replaced it in the 19th century. The furnaces with their water-powered bellows were greedy and sometimes the woods were devastated. It is possible to find the flat platforms or 'pitsteads' where the wood was carefully stacked for the slow controlled burn which was necessary to produce the best charcoal. The commonest broadleaved trees are as they were always, sessile oak, birch, holly, alder, cherry, crabapple, rowan and wych elm. The conifers were Scots pine, juniper and yew. A lot of what is now seen has been planted in past centuries, and some of the best mixtures – often at their most colourful in autumn – were planted by new landowners who were not all the 'tasteless' philistines whom Wordsworth condemned.

The extent of the managed broadleaved woodlands has diminished in an age when woods, and traditional craftsmanship, have come increasingly to be regarded as disposable. Sometimes they have been replaced by alien regimented conifer plantations which produce a quick crop of straight timber. However, many of the remaining deciduous woodlands are now in caring ownership, including that of the National Trust and the National Park Authority. The

Forestry Commission is now actively concerned and there are good hopes for their survival. These woods are one of the few remaining habitats of the red squirrel. Fortunately, the alien grey squirrels have never crossed the natural barriers of Morecambe Bay and the eastern moorlands to oust our less harmful and more handsome animal. The red's ideal habitat is pine wood with hazel undercover. They are extremely shy, but occasionally appear at winter bird tables.

Lakeland deer

The small roe deer inhabit nearly every wood. This, surely the most beautiful of our native animals, so delicately formed and graceful, has an uneasy existence. They are often road casualties. They are persecuted because of the damage they do to unfenced gardens. Their fawns are picked up under the mistaken impression that they have been 'abandoned', and without their mother's attention can soon die. Roe often move about in small family groups, while the largest of our mammals, the red deer, are herd animals. They have lived in the southern Lake District since long before human settlement. A stag here can stand about four feet six inches high with the antler spread another two feet high and three feet wide. The better-fed woodland stag is heavier than the stag adapted to the eastern fells. Red deer herds are sometimes seen on the woodland fringes where they emerge to graze. The nightly roaring of the challenging stags at the rut, and sometimes the clash of antlers as they fight, are the most exciting sounds of the woods.

A red deer stag with his harem of hinds. The stag barks to pronounce his superiority and to ward off rivals. The mating season lasts from mid September to October; for the rest of the year stags and hinds live apart

Masters of the air

The monarchs of the fell skies are undoubtedly the ravens. Sometimes their 'cronk' is the only sound to break the intense silence of the high places, and their acrobatics in spring, perhaps casting a twig away and then recatching it, are joys that can be shared. Claimants to the throne are golden eagles, which have returned to the Lake District after an absence of 200 years. Go purposely to see them and they will sit still for hours, merged into the background of a crag

Above and below left: a golden eagle, carrying prey, being mobbed by ravens. There are only a few pairs of golden eagles in the Lake District, but the honking call of the raven is commonly heard

Above: a buzzard. These handsome birds are common throughout the Lake District. They are most often seen gliding high in the sky on outstretched, motionless, wings

ledge. But it is pure delight to see them unexpectedly soaring in the air currents on the mountain edges. In recent years we have seen the return of the peregrine falcons. The Lake District is one of Europe's major breeding grounds of this most beautiful of all the hawks.

So well do high peaks, low fells and valleys blend and harmonise that it is very difficult to define clear ecological zones. Where for instance could you place the buzzard? Buzzards are common everywhere and are often mistaken for eagles. Like eagles they are masters of the air current, hardly moving their broad wings. Buzzards are equally at home among the fells or over the valley tree tops, and their plaintive cry is an essential part of the Lake District's character.

Purple saxifrage. This is one of several species of alpine plant that can be found in rocky places where grazing sheep cannot reach

Wild flowers in the wilderness

In moist places on the fells, on steep crags, and in deep shady ravines – anywhere the hungry sheep cannot reach – in such places it is possible to find examples of Lakeland's living botanical history. The isolated fragments of the ancient forests' flora survive here: primrose, foxglove, dog's mercury, bluebell, wood sorrel, anemone, stitchwort, lady fern and male fern and polypody. Trees grow where they can, sometimes seemingly from the rock itself. There are plants in the Lake District whose story is very different from that of the forest-living flowers. Higher in the inaccessible wet areas, where seeping springs have gradually dissolved minerals from the hard rocks, are less common plants like the purple, golden, and starry saxifrages. In high places can be found rare alpines left from the Ice Age. These are plants that can survive on thin soils and withstand extremes of temperature and drought. Lichens, mosses and liverworts are the only plants which can survive on the bare rocks of the most exposed sites. Typical plants of the grassy, rock-strewn mountainsides are heath bedstraw, moss campion and tormentil. Ferns abound. The mountain parsley fern, almost a luminous green in spring, is found among crags everywhere and grows in no other place in Britain so profusely. In the deeper soils there are vast areas of bracken, the curse of the farmer as the stuff is inedible by stock. Yet lovers of fine scenery also love bracken for its changing colours – light green in spring; and in the autumn a magnificent display of yellow, orange and brown.

Beside the waters

The lake and river margins are often excellent habitats rich in vegetation. Such places are perhaps at their best in summer when the banks are glowing with purple loosestrife, yellow flag, cow parsley, ragged robin, valerian; and heavy with the scent of meadowsweet. Metal-bright dragon flies and damsel flies – red and blue and green – flash in the sunlight. That marvellous bird of our upland rivers, the dipper, with the lovely liquid song and its subaqua walk is often present. Otters? They come and go like ghosts. Once they were numerous and otter hunting was a popular sport. Now maybe there is too much human activity. But it could happen that in the beck just off the beaten track you might see the bubbles rising, the curve of the shining body, and glimpse that lively little whiskered face.

Only the shallower lakes such as Esthwaite Water, Rydal Water, and Loweswater are 'eutrophic' waters, that is rich in the nutrients which support an abundance of plant and animal

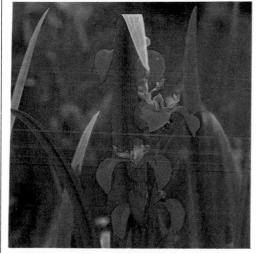

Plants like the yellow flag are found in watery places where there are plenty of nutrients

growth. Anglers may not be too enthusiastic about rich habitats unless they like coarse fishing, but the perch and pike can give good sport. Sea trout, brown trout, and salmon favour the clearer water of the deeper lakes and rivers. One fish peculiar to the district is the char, a deepwater trout. Windermere potted char was once a delicacy much sought after by the gentry of past times. Two rare relics of the Ice Age survive uniquely in Lakeland waters. In Ullswater there are shoals of schelly, sometimes described as 'freshwater herring' though not related. They used to be netted in large quantities. The vendace is another rare whitefish. It is found only in Bassenthwaite and Derwent Water.

Creatures great and small

Of large animals on the hills the common fox is the sole native if one discounts the seasonal movements of red deer. Pine martens once occupied the fells but they are now almost certainly absent. There are occasional rumours of sightings, but the first-hand observer is now an endangered species.

The predators, particularly of rabbits and hares, are the stoats and weasels. They often make their homes in drystone walls. In winter there are frequent sightings of 'ermine' stoats, the animals shedding their brown coat for a creamy white but still with the black end to the tail. Drystone walls too give shelter to reptiles such as the common lizard and the harmless slow-worm, which is often mistaken for a snake but is in fact a legless lizard prone to shedding its tail when attacked. Adders are common. They are shy reptiles and will rush for cover on approach. They are recognised by their zig-zag striped back and the V on their heads. Adder bites are rare and not usually serious. The bitten are invariably people who have foolishly cornered them and picked them up; or more rarely have stood on them as they bask in the spring sunshine still sluggish after hibernation.

Purists among naturalists after a superficial observation of the Lake District might suggest that the hills are too bleak, the lakes too pure, the soils too acid. However, it is impossible to generalise, for the district offers the explorer a great wealth of interest; from liverworts to oak trees; tiny goldcrests to golden eagles; pigmy shrews to twelve-pointer stags. The great shaping of the Lake District back in geological times produced an enormous range of habitats, the depth, height and breadth of which could never be wholly appreciated in a single lifetime.

Left: a vendace, one of Britain's rarest fishes

Below: a male and female char in their spawning colours

Dorothy and William Wordsworth

Literary Lakeland

The lives and works of Dorothy and William Wordsworth shine with such a dazzling light over the literary landscape of Lakeland that we are apt to ignore the other rich associations with fine writers – past and present. True, one of the most memorised poems in English – *Daffodils* (or, 'I wandered lonely as a cloud . . .') – was inspired by a scene on the shores of Ullswater, but the same hills and dales, lakes and tarns, which inspired the Wordsworths, have also nurtured and stimulated generations of poets, novelists and essayists. To the Wordsworths belongs the enviable distinction of having been born in Cumbria; most of their long lives were spent among the hills and dales of Lakeland, and their adjacent graves in the churchyard of Grasmere – the very heart of Lakeland – are among the most visited literary shrines in the world. Pay homage by all means to their memory, but be sure not to neglect the other fascinating associations the area has to offer.

Naturally Wordsworth's contemporaries in Lakeland spring first to mind – especially his fellow Lake Poets, Samuel Taylor Coleridge and Poet Laureate Robert Southey, as well as that poet in prose, Thomas De Quincey. All three spent a good deal of time in the company of the Wordsworths, and helped to establish the Lake District as a desirable place to live in or visit. Among the distinguished visitors were Walter Scott, John Keats, Charlotte Brontë, Charles Dickens, Nathaniel Hawthorne, and Lord Alfred Tennyson. Others were so enchanted with the area that they made their homes in the Lakes: Matthew Arnold, John Ruskin, Beatrix Potter, Arthur Ransome, and Hugh Walpole.

Modern writers

Today the literary tradition continues, with many modern writers having their main or second homes among the lakes and hills or at least drawing on their Lakeland experiences for much of their inspiration. Among modern writers Norman Nicholson reigns supreme as the most impressive voice of the region. Many of the novels of Melvyn Bragg are set in his home area of Wigton and that vast tract of land between the northern fringes of Lakeland and the Scottish border. Best-selling author Richard Adams set his *Plague Dogs* in the Duddon Valley, and the spell-binding autobiography *The Shining Levels*, by John Wyatt, is set in the peaceful woodlands south-east of Lake Windermere. Present or past or famous or neglected, all give the literary traveller a wealth of riches from which to arrange a reading itinerary.

A Wordsworth tour

There can be no doubt that the best introduction to Literary Lakeland is to follow in the steps of Wordsworth, for his life and work, directly or indirectly, is the source and inspiration of most of the finest writing about Lakeland. Both William and his sister Dorothy were born in Cockermouth, that half-forgotten market town on the far north-western fringe of the National Park. Their father's imposing Georgian house, still the most impressive façade in the town, is open to the public and protected by the National Trust.

William briefly attended the school in the town before going to Dame Birkett's school in Penrith, although most of his education was at the Grammar School in Hawkshead, an Elizabethan foundation which at that time enjoyed a high reputation for scholarship. The poet's initials are carved in one of the desks.

Grasmere and Rydal

The more mountainous scenery around Grasmere and Rydal was the setting for most of the Wordsworths' lives. For it was to Grasmere in December 1799, just as the century turned, that William and Dorothy settled at Dove Cottage, later to be joined by their childhood companion, Mary Hutchinson, who married William in 1802. In these early years at Dove Cottage Samuel Taylor Coleridge was a frequent visitor, having settled at Greta Hall, Keswick with his brother-in-law Robert Southey. De Quincey, too, was a frequent visitor and eventually made his own home at Dove Cottage after the increasing Wordsworth family made the house overcrowded. The first move to Allan Bank proved unsatisfactory and they moved again, to the Rectory opposite Grasmere Church. Here tragedy struck the family, two of their small children dying within a few months of each other in 1812. The front windows of the Rectory look directly onto the graves and the proximity of the churchyard cast a gloom over the whole household. A further move, their last, was vital and

Below: daffodils and spring light at Ullswater.
Right: Wordsworth's birthplace at Cockermouth

they settled on Rydal Mount, a mile and a half to the south on the road to Ambleside.

Allan Bank and the Rectory, though not open to the public, can easily be viewed from public ways: Dove Cottage is open six and a half days a week, and the guided tour of the tiny rooms is an essential experience for Wordsworth fans.

Rydal Mount, too, is open and as well as the house containing furnishings, paintings, portraits and such homely reminders of their daily lives as ice skates and picnic boxes, the gardens which William so patiently laid out have now been restored to their former glory.

All around Rydal and Grasmere are tracks and footpaths which the Wordsworths habitually walked – William composed most of his verse out of doors. A favourite summertime activity was to take a boat onto Grasmere and row out to the island for a picnic – still a highly recommended jaunt for discriminating visitors keen to escape the roads and traffic.

Dove Cottage – most famous of Wordsworth's homes

The famous daffodils

Two other spots should not be missed in order to complete a Wordsworth tour. On the shores of Ullswater at Gowbarrow is the woodland where the famous daffodils were sighted. William was not in fact wandering alone, he was with Dorothy, and it was she who recorded the scene in her journal. Only two years later did William write the poem, and he clearly drew heavily on his sister's fresh and vivid description of those hosts of golden daffodils. Today alas, though the scenery is superb, there are few daffodils to be seen here. Those in search of Wordsworth's images must content themselves with a stop at Dora's Field just below Rydal Mount next to the church. Here, in a field which William bought and planted himself, we can be certain of seeing in early spring an excellent show of flowers worthy of William's poem:

> Ten thousand saw I at a glance,
> Tossing their heads in sprightly dance.

This pretty scene is perhaps a more fitting climax to the Wordsworth tour than the more common pilgrimage to the graves in Grasmere churchyard, with the tiny headstones of young Catherine and Thomas, and the poignant memorial to brother John, drowned in a shipwreck on the Dorset coast.

Samuel Taylor Coleridge

Coleridge and Southey

When Samuel Taylor Coleridge was introduced to the Lakeland scenery by William and brother John on a walking tour, he immediately fell in love with the area, though he wrote little poetry relating specifically to the Lakes. His notebooks and letters, however, abound with excited descriptions of the scenery and his accounts of his walks are full of joy and exhilaration. Indeed his report of his ascent of Scafell is one of the recognised classics of mountaineering literature, and shows Coleridge as a pioneer fell-walker. He lived for a time at Greta Hall, Keswick, with his brother-in-law Robert Southey, a prolific poet in his day but now largely neglected. His fame today rests on being Poet Laureate before Wordsworth accepted the honour, and for writing the tale of *The Three Bears*. Southey's memorial at Crosthwaite Church has been restored by the Brazilian government, a testimony to the high esteem in which that country holds him as their nation's first historian.

Just south of Keswick is Castlerigg Stone Circle, impressive both as an ancient monument

Robert Southey (above) was a prolific poet, but today is most remembered for his lines about the Lodore Falls (below). They begin: 'How does the water/Come down at Lodore?'

and for its setting, with mountain views in all directions. The circle provided Keats with the inspiration for his description in *Hyperion*:

> ... like a dismal cirque
> Of Druid stone, upon a forlorn moor,
> When the chill rain begins at shut of eve,
> In dull November ...

But see the circle on a bright summer morning, or on a soft balmy evening, and you may regret that Keats did not also celebrate this spot in its more benignly mysterious mood.

A Tennyson connection

Further north, on the shores of Bassenthwaite Lake, Tennyson gained inspiration for the lake imagery in *Morte D'Arthur* during a stay with his friends the Speddings at their fine home at Mirehouse – one of the most recent literary houses to be opened to the public. The ancient church of St Bega is a short walk from the house, standing alone like a stranded ship in the lakeside fields. The building has recently been sensitively restored and visiting this quiet corner of Lakeland it is possible to feel the full power and force of Tennyson's extraordinary story:

> Then bold Sir Bedivere uplifted him,
> Sir Bedivere the last of all his knights,
> And bore him to a chapel in the fields
> A broken chancel with a broken cross,
> That stood on a dark straight of barren land
> On one side lay the Ocean, and on one
> Lay a great water, and the moon was full.

Inspiring mountains

Connections with other eminent 19th-century figures can be found in another half-forgotten corner of Lakeland, off the main road between Ambleside and Rydal in an area known as Under Loughrigg. Here, at Fox How, by the banks of the River Rothay, the poet and critic Matthew Arnold lived in this solid house. He is better known for his poetry of the Oxfordshire countryside, and for being the son of Dr Arnold of *Tom Brown's Schooldays* fame, but he was deeply attached to the Lake District, and it is fitting that after his death his friends should have erected a memorial stone close to the church at Wythburn, near Thirlmere, marking the spot where he began a favourite walk to Harrop Tarn. Carved into the stone are Arnold's lines which capture the atmosphere that all fell-walkers relish:

> And now, in front, behold outspread
> These upper regions we must tread,
> Mild hollows, and clear heathy swells,
> The cheerful silence of the fells.

Wythburn Church itself is well worth visiting not only for its obvious picturesque qualities but for the interesting exhibition it contains on the history of the immediate area, which includes extracts from various poems about the tiny church. From Wythburn begins a popular route onto Helvellyn which Wordsworth, Walter Scott and Humphry Davy once climbed together, resulting in the two poets each versifying the moving story of the young man who died on the mountain and was guarded by his faithful dog. Scott brings out the drama of the ascent:

> As I climbed the dark slopes of mighty Helvellyn
> The torrents were roaring, the eagles were yelling . . .

A few miles to the north is another association with Scott, for St John's-in-the-Vale is the setting for his *Bridal of Triermain*: a highly imaginative story involving all the elements of far-off legend, with King Arthur and Guinevere and a purely fictitious castle perched on the so-called Castle Rock of St John, so named because earlier, fanciful travellers imagined that the natural configuration of the crags was in fact a castle.

More recently written historical romances can be found in the novels of Hugh Walpole, enjoying a revival as the result of the television adaptations of the Herries Chronicles, realistically set in the valley of Borrowdale. Walpole's house at Manesty, on the south-west side of Derwent Water is not open to the public; however, the gardens are occasionally opened for charity. Walpole's stories are characterised by highly accurate descriptions of selected locations which his devoted admirers delight in tracking down – such as Judith Paris' house by Watendlath Tarn.

In search of Mrs Tiggywinkle and Captain Flint

On the north-west shore of Derwent Water the gardens of Lingholm are regularly opened by the present owners Lord and Lady Rochdale. Here Beatrix Potter stayed, and her children's stories often have authentic and recognisable backgrounds. The shores and islands of Derwent Water, for instance, clearly figure in *The Tale of Squirrel Nutkin*. Beatrix Potter's most famous house though, is Hill Top, at Sawrey, and close by, the Tower Bank Arms is clearly recognisable to readers of *The Tale of Jemima Puddleduck*. Nearby Esthwaitewater was the home of Jeremy Fisher, and children and adults alike can spend many hours tracking down the settings of these immortal tales.

To many older children the Lake District is not Potter Country but Ransomeland, for Arthur Ransome's *Swallows and Amazons* combines elements of Coniston Water and Windermere. Imaginatively convincing on his pages, but frustratingly difficult to locate on the ground, his readers have to accept that there is often no very precise location for the adventures of Titty, Nancy, Roger and Captain Flint. Wildcat Island is often thought to be Rampsholme on Windermere, but Peel Island on Coniston Water is more likely

The flags of the 'Swallows and Amazons'

to be the island Ransome had in mind.

Coniston Water is also where we can see the former home of John Ruskin. This is Brantwood, a truly fascinating house enjoying quite one of the most impressive views in the Lake District. Brantwood is open to the public, a fascinating and extraordinary testimony to the roving mind of one of Britain's most famous 19th-century art critics, who found time for social reform, poetry and painting.

Glance in any Lakeland bookshop – the area is well served by them – and you will find ample evidence that the long and honourable literary traditions of the Lake District continue: the thrilling and unputdownable *Bride of Lowther Fell*, Margaret Forster's yarn set in the northern fells; John Wyatt's inspired and uplifting *The Shining Levels*; and Norman Nicholson's unforgettable poems, drawing their strength not only from the hills but also from the life of the industrial area around his Millom home. All of these are part of a rolecall of names and works stretching back to the poems and person of Wordsworth.

Fell Walking

The countryside of the Lake District is undoubtedly among the finest in the British Isles. Drive through it and the beauty of the landscape cannot fail to impress. That, for many, is enough; and of course to explore the Lake District by car enables the holidaymaker with only a week or two at his disposal to see a great many of the Lakes' attractions. But to walk in the fresh Cumbrian air away from the crowds and the restrictions of metalled roads is considerably more rewarding.

There is no need to be an athlete or a mountaineer – there are paths to suit everyone. But there are a few ground rules which should be adhered to.

An essential requirement is an ability to read a map – not a hard skill to acquire, as every map carries a 'legend' which lists and interprets all the symbols on the map. Equally important is the need to be properly prepared. Comfortable footwear with a good-grip sole is the main essential. Some choose well-fitting wellingtons; but they can be uncomfortably hot after a time. Light waterproofs are the next need, then plenty of food, and of course a map and compass. Do not be too ambitious when planning the walk – 2½ miles (4 km) per hour is a good speed to plan for over more or less level ground.

Fell walking

Exploring the Lake District on foot may involve sampling the delights of fell walking, which is a quite different proposition from walking in the gentler lowlands. Too many who have ventured onto the heights ill-prepared have found the experience exhausting and worrying; and a few have found it painful. The Lake District mountain rescue teams, volunteers all, turn out to over 130 rescues each year. Here more people have to be searched for on the mountains, or carried down off them, than anywhere else in Britain. This does not by any means give the whole accident picture. Very many minor casualties find their own way down, or are helped by passers-by. Ninety-five per cent of these incidents could have been avoided. The accident rate is not high here because more walkers are careless in the Lake District than anywhere else. It is just that far, far more people are attracted by the open-to-all freedom of hundreds of square miles of superb mountain summits. The small minority who get it wrong are still too many. It is not the intention to dissuade people from walking on the fells if they want to. Nor it it intended to suggest that fell walking is the best and ultimate adventure for everyone. Many walkers will find everything they want in the lower hills and valleys, the rivers and lakesides.

The weather

Conditions on the high fells bear no resemblance to the conditions in the valley. The difference can be extreme. When it is mild spring weather at low levels at Easter, bleak mid-winter is still in possession of the summits. One of the worst possible conditions on the fells is gale-force driven rain. Without proper equipment it can be lethal and it happens very often in July and August. No one should be on the fells in those conditions, nor any other bad conditions. Seek the weather forecast first. It is taped on Windermere 5151, the National Park's service. Be prepared to modify your plans, no matter how frustrating, if the forecast is bad.

It should go without saying that winter fell walking is only for those with a lot of fell walking experience. When daylight hours are short a map-reading error can mean being benighted.

On footwear

It is quite possible for a lot of people to traverse the fells in wellies or sandals given the right conditions of dryness underfoot. These conditions are not normal on the fells. It is also true that heavy and expensive mountaineering boots are not needed except in winter snows. Light boots with well-cleated soles are recommended. Get used to the boots first on wet rock or loose gravel or steep grass, before trying them out on the fells.

Windproofs and waterproofs

Cold wind is a serious hazard on the fells. A windproof is essential and it can be carried in a rucksack until needed. If it is also the essential waterproof, that saves carrying two garments. Most people go for the dual-purpose, but condensation on the inside of 'non-breathing' material can be a problem. There are now garments made of magical materials claiming to solve this. You may need to take out a mortgage to buy them. Light waterproof overtrousers are also needed – cold wet knees are hard to cope with.

Warm clothing

Warm clothing such as a sweater, hat and gloves is needed. If it is cold enough to wear woollies at low level some extras should also be put in the sack to prepare for the inevitable big drop in temperature on the heights.

Equipment

Map and compass and the know-how to use them are the first essentials. The rucksack should be large enough. A small tightly-packed bag is a nasty lumpy burden. Take plenty of food including extras for emergencies. It is not necessary to carry water on the Lake District fells as the high-level becks are pure (but cold – and can cause stomach complaints if indulged in too often). A flask of tea or coffee is a good idea. A simple first aid kit should be in the sack; and a torch – just in case unavoidable delay means a descent in the dark. (Without it a descent might be impossible.) For emergencies most experienced walkers carry two light extras: a whistle (six blasts at intervals summons assistance), and a large polythene bag big enough to crawl into, or to slide an injured person into, for an emergency shelter.

The plan

The route plan is all-important. A poor one, or a too ambitious one, is a main cause of serious trouble. Plan to walk at 2½ miles (4 km) per hour; but examine the contours and add one hour for every 1,500 feet (450 metres) to be ascended. To this add refreshment and taking-photographs-time, or slow-walker-in-party time. Best to keep some time in hand too in case of problems. A 'B' plan is also necessary. This is the essential foul-weather route alternative. Leave details of the final plan with somone at base wherever that is. This is very essential for lone walkers. If you break an ankle someone needs to know where to look for you. If you are delayed or descend into the wrong valley a telephone call could save a possible unnecessary rescue call-out. The police, who initiate rescues, would like to know. There are too many times when rescue teams turn out on the cold night fell to look for someone who is snug by the fire in some dale bar, and has not bothered to tell anyone of a change of plan.

The walk

The best comment on safety I heard was from an Everest mountaineer: 'The difference between a mountaineer and a novice is that the mountaineer knows when to turn back.' Do not be hesitant at making the decision to modify or shorten routes for safety reasons. Group or family leaders have a responsibility. Groups should not be split up but should journey at the speed of the slowest member. Keep to sensible routes. Walking the fells should never be confused with rock climbing. Rock faces and gullies are for devotees of a different sport.

The emergency

The procedure if one locates an incident is to work out the position carefully on the map, write down the map reference, and either take it or send it with someone to the nearest telephone. A 999 call to the police with details of the incident will start the rescue.

In winter

If there is snow on the hills an ice axe and know-how to use it is essential. In extreme conditions crampons may be needed. The phone-in weather service gives details of winter fell-top conditions.

The above advice is sensible and its observance does not involve heavy expense. For more specific advice the National Park Ranger Service (Barclays Bank Chambers, Crescent Rd, Windermere) is available. Youth leaders can obtain help from the National Park Youth & Schools Service, Brockhole, Windermere.

Having digested this advice relax and enjoy the walk. The fell walker is mainly after two things: complete freedom of the open air, and adventure. The safety rules do not restrict freedom and there are no National Park rangers hiding behind rocks ready to jump out on those who are not strictly observing them. Adventure suggests an element of uncertainty. But the environment should provide those delights of surprise. The wise take ability and experience into account and should heed the advice of Edward Whymper, the 19th-century pioneer of mountaineering who learned by some grim mistakes: 'Climb if you will, but remember that courage and strength are nought without prudence and that a momentary negligence may destroy the happiness of a lifetime. Do nothing in haste, look well to each step and from the beginning, think what might be the end.'

If the right decisions were made on the walk the end should be a hot shower, a good meal, a satisfied feeling of achievement, and a happy memory.

Right: walking is the best way to explore the Lake District. This view is from Silverhow, looking down on Grasmere

Below: fell walking in winter is exhilarating, but the correct equipment is essential

Traditional Sports

Long before tourists came to the Lake District the dalesmen were chasing foxes across the fells and wrestling on the village greens. Fell racing and hound trailing came much later – although both these events were staged at the first recorded Grasmere Sports meeting in 1852 – and these four preoccupations of the dalesmen are still the principal traditional sports of the district, all born in the fell country and still rarely seen outside it. Note the mountain association in three of these four activities, and even the wrestling in the specialised Cumberland and Westmorland style, today held against the backcloth of the fells, at one time took place on the summit of High Street. You need strong legs and arms, good lungs and sure balance for all these pursuits – the men who lay the trails for the hounds cover the same rough mountain course that the animals have to follow – and the mountains breed such men. The traditional sports of Lakeland, then, are a heritage from the hills, for the dalesman has never been greatly attracted to the lakes and the lake sports. The Royal Windermere Yacht Club is more than 120 years old and today there are motorboating, water-skiing and swimming races, but these things are not bred in the dalesman. One can

imagine him looking on, with some wonder and amusement, at the regattas on Derwentwater and Windermere in the early 19th century, but probably begrudging the time spent away from the hunting or the wrestling.

Hunting and huntsmen
Fox hunting is the main interest, almost the obsession, of the dalesman during the winter months and, increasingly, an attraction for visitors who view the chase through binoculars from cars parked on mountain roads and join in the merriment at the inn later. There are six mountain packs covering the whole of Lakeland and well to the east of the Shap Fells road. The hunts, often two or three times a week, are advertised in the local newspapers. Hunting in the fells has little in common with the fashionable sport of the shires, for the dalesman hunts on foot and only the huntsman wears the red coat. Killing foxes is just another job like keeping down the crows or repairing fences, for foxes slink down from the heights to prey on the poultry and young lambs; but the farmers and shepherds are out for sport as well, and a kill before breakfast, before the sun has ruined the scent, is common enough. Fell hunting is a hard game and you need to know the ways of a fox and have a feeling for the lie of mountain country, besides sound limbs and good lungs, to be up with the kill. To some it seems a sickening business, chasing a beautiful animal to the death, but it is necessary to keep down the number of foxes and it is arguable that hunting is the most practical way. The fox is normally killed in an instant by a snap from the leading hound, and the Lakeland packs do not break up their victim, which is often hung in state on a farmhouse door – an honoured foe and perhaps an example to his fellows.

Above: a fell runner making the headlong descent of Wasdale Head

Right: traditional Lakeland wrestling at one of the region's many shows

Far left: hounds of the Coniston pack with their huntsman

Below: they're off! The start of a hound trail

Below right: fell runners clearing a wall at the famous Grasmere Sports

The legendary John Peel is mostly remembered in the song written by his old friend John Woodcock Graves. His hunting country was largely to the north of what is now the National Park. He often hunted the flatter land on horseback, and he was a flamboyant character rather than a particularly heroic figure. Several later, less-publicised fell huntsmen, notably Tommy Dobson of the Eskdale and Ennerdale hunt, Billy Porter of the same pack, the great Joe Bowman of the Ullswater, Joe Wear who succeeded him and Anthony Chapman of the Coniston, probably all exceeded Peel's records of kills and were, in some ways, more interesting men. But present-day hunting owes something to John Peel, for some of his hounds were used for breeding the forebears of the present Blencathra pack which hunts the Keswick country.

Hound trailing

When the hounds are resting from their hard work of the winter the dalesman turns to his summer absorption with dogs – the Lake District sport of hound trailing. Trail hounds are basically fox hounds but specially bred and trained into sleeker, lighter animals capable of considerable speed and endurance over rough mountain ground. Hound trailing can provide some fine spectacles – the excitement of the 'slip', the yelping surge over the first stone wall, the wonderful sight of scurrying specks coursing along a distant shoulder of fell and the thrill of a close-fought finish – but undoubtedly the betting is the principal attraction. The hounds are groomed and cosseted like racehorses and although, doubtless, their owners show them affection, they are really the stock-in-trade of the itinerant bookie. Every sports meeting, agricultural show and sheepdog trial has its hound trail – generally two or three in an afternoon – and there are trails nearly every day in summer in one part of the district or another. The sport is highly organised with a ruling body founded as long ago as 1906, and the corruption that was formerly a feature of the sport – hounds substituted, drugged or even taken part of the way by car – has now been stamped out. But to some it may seem a pity that a potentially fascinating outdoor spectacle is really little more than a gamble.

Cumberland wrestling

But wrestling in the Cumberland and Westmorland style has little or no attraction for the betting man and although there are tales of faked contests in the past it is nowadays one of the cleanest of sports. The best man wins and the one who throws all his opponents becomes the champion of the meeting at his weight. And the best wrestlers, at specially selected competitions, become 'world champions' in this particular style – an honour that many an 18-year-old farm lad from the dales has been able to claim. It looks a simple sport but, in fact, is highly technical. The round ends when one man is down, and there is no need for both shoulders to be touching the ground; if both fall together the winner is the one on top. Most visitors understand little or nothing of the many types of attack and the curious jargon, but the secret of the game is to tempt your opponent into a position of apparent security and then quickly to get him off balance. Mere strength is by no means the whole of it.

The best wrestlers, however, seem well-built and sturdy, and the heavyweights are often very big men indeed. Perhaps the outstanding man in the long history of the sport – probably up to 300 years – was the great George Steadman, who died at Brough in 1904 – a powerful but paunchy man who measured 51½ inches round the chest but probably even more round the waist. He won the heavyweight contest at Grasmere on 14 occasions, represented England at many international competitions, collected enough cups and trophies to stock a jeweller's shop and probably made more money out of the game than anybody else. One or two others have since equalled or exceeded his total of Grasmere wins but Steadman who looked, with his bald, smiling face and white side-whiskers, rather like a bishop, remains the personality of the sport.

The traditional wrestling costume must be mentioned – white vest and hose with gaily embroidered trunks – and there are usually competitions for the best costume, generally judged by ladies. Wrestling in the fell country is a fine, manly sport and the sight of sunburned dalesmen, dressed in white, struggling good-naturedly on a circle of green turf set among the hills remains a picture of the best of old England.

Fell racing

The beginnings of fell racing in the Lakes – or guides racing, as it is sometimes called – have long been forgotten but it was already an established sport at Grasmere in the 1850s. Here, for many visitors, is the main attraction of the dales sports, for this is sheer spectacle throughout – the long climb up through the bracken and over the rocks to the flag on the summit of the nearest fell and then the breakneck dash down the fellside, over walls, across slippery slopes and into the arena, while the band strikes up 'See the conquering hero comes'. Most of the outstanding fell runners, with many wins at the main sports meetings at Grasmere and Ambleside to their credit, have been young farmers, farm hands or shepherds to whom this peak of physical fitness has presented a worthwhile challenge. Here is another traditional sport where the bookmaker has intruded but the game is clean enough, with the race in full view through binoculars, and the honour of winning at an important meeting highly prized. Some champions are better on the climb, others on the wild descent, and the first man to the summit is not always the first to breast the tape. Even youngsters of ten or twelve have their own races and they often become the great champions of later years.

These, then, are the main traditional sports of Lakeland – most of them to be seen at a score of summer sports meetings but, notably, at Grasmere on the nearest Thursday to 20 August and at Ambleside on the last Thursday in July. But there is one more traditional 'sport' of the fell country – the ancient gurning, or grinning, competitions most often associated with the old Crab Fair at Egremont. You simply place your head through a horse-collar and the winner is the man who pulls the ugliest face. It has been reported of one former champion gurner that the first time he won the prize he had not really entered the competition at all but had been merely 'following the efforts of the others with interest and sympathy'. But perhaps this 'sport' should be placed in the same category as the competitions at Wasdale Head and elsewhere to find the best liar in the district.

Gazetteer

▲ Whinlatter Pass

Each entry in this Gazetteer has the atlas
page number on which the place can be
found and its National Grid reference
included under the heading. An
explanation of how to use the National
Grid is given on page 68.

▲ Every year on the first Saturday in July children process through the streets of Ambleside carrying 'bearings' decorated with flowers and rushes which are later placed in the church where a service is held

MAP REF: 82NY4020

When waterfalls were all on the Victorian itinerary, a visit to Aira Force, in an idyllic wooded gorge on the west side of Ullswater, was obligatory. There was a suitable

Aira Force tumbles down a lovely wooded ravine in which bridges have been built as viewpoints ▼

AMBLESIDE

MAP REF: 87NY3704

Ambleside is a major Lake District centre, lying in a strategic position on the main north - south road (A591). It is a good base for a touring, walking or climbing holiday and has many facilities and shops.

The Romans showed their appreciation of Ambleside's strategic attractions in AD79 when they built *Galava* fort at Borrans near Waterhead.

Granted its charter as a market town in 1650, Ambleside has remnants of the 17th century, such as the tiny Bridge House over the Stock Ghyll, built as a summer house for the former Ambleside Hall. It is now owned by the National Trust, who opened it as their first information centre in 1956.

St Mary's Church has a 180ft spire, unusual in the Lake District. It contains a mural depicting the ancient rushbearing ceremony painted by Gordon Ransome, a student of the Royal College of Art during World War II, when the college was evacuated to Ambleside. The annual ceremony is held on the first Saturday in July, when children carry rushes through the town. It dates from medieval times, when the rushes used as flooring in the church were renewed each year.

The area is rich in historical and literary associations. William Wordsworth and his sister used to walk into Ambleside from Grasmere (see page 36) to get their post and later, in 1813, when Wordsworth became Distributor of Stamps for Westmorland, he had his office here.

The writer Harriet Martineau lived at The Knoll from 1835 to 1876. In 1912 the Armitt sisters, who also lived in the town, left their unique and valuable collection of local history books for the use of students (now housed in a special section of the Ambleside Library).

The historic centre of Ambleside is now a conservation area. Stock Ghyll Waterfall used to serve several mills. The Old Mill on North Road has a good reproduction waterwheel.

Traditional Lakeland sports are held at Ambleside on the Thursday before the first Monday in August, and the traditionally renowned sheepdog trials take place in Rydal Park. Boat and steamer trips are available from Waterhead (see under Windermere, page 64).

legend attached to the place with all the sentimental ingredients: noble knight, faithful lady, tragic meeting, death scene. Wordsworth's version is told in 'The Somnambulist'. Whether the Aira Beck is in force or not, the setting is attractive. It is in the care of the National Trust and there is a car park and café on site.

ASHNESS
MAP REF: 80NY2619

On the steeply cragged and wooded south-east side of Derwent Water, Ashness Woods crown the unclassified road from Borrowdale to Watendlath. Here there are two of the most famous Lakeland viewpoints. Where the road crosses Barrow Beck, Ashness Bridge provides the artist or photographer with all requirements: foreground arched bridge, background of lake and mountains. South of this the road runs close to a cliff edge and Surprise View gives an airy prospect over Derwent Water to Bassenthwaite lake and the north-western fells.

A familiar Lakeland view – Ashness Bridge with Derwent Water and Derwent Fells providing the background ▼

BASSENTHWAITE LAKE
MAP REF: 73NY2026

Bassenthwaite Lake, four miles long, is the fourth largest area of water in the National Park and is in the ownership of the National Park Authority which gives priority to the protection and enhancement of the nature conservation interests of the lake and the surrounding area. Power boats are not permitted. It is in the less dramatic scenery of Skiddaw Slate, so lacks overhanging cliffs and close viewpoints. From Skiddaw, or from Thornwaite Forest on the west, the views are memorable if remote. The west side is marred by the close proximity of the A66, but there are several public access areas. Bassenthwaite village is to the north-east, away from the shore, but the old Bassenthwaite Church, dedicated to St Bega, is by the lake, signed from the A591 but reached by a track at its last stage. The scene here, before the church was restored in the 19th century, was described in Tennyson's *Idylls of the King*. Tennyson was a frequent visitor to nearby Mirehouse (see page 48) and southwards on the shore line, on Mirehouse property, an inscribed stone marks the place where the poet was inspired to compose his lines about the last hours of King Arthur.

The lake is fed notably by the River Derwent from neighbouring Derwent Water, and shares with the latter lake the habitat of the rare freshwater whitefish, the vendace.

BLACK COMBE
MAP REF: 90SD1385

Black Combe, an expansive dome of Skiddaw Slate rising to 1970ft, is at the south-western extremity of the Lakeland fells. Because of its remoteness, and its approach over a large area of relatively uninteresting moorland, it is rather neglected by walkers, yet its views out to sea to the Isle of Man, to the Scottish hills and, clarity allowing, to Ireland and North Wales, are magnificent. Wordsworth enthused. He wrote 'View from the top of Black Combe' in 1813:

> . . . the amplest range
> Of unobstructed prospect
> may be seen
> That British ground
> commands

BLENCATHRA
MAP REF: 74NY3227

Blencathra or 'Saddleback' (2847ft) is eastern sister to Skiddaw, and from St Johns in the Vale to the south, which sees its steepest sides, it is

every inch a mountain. From a fell-walker's viewpoint it is far superior to Skiddaw, offering a variety of terrain. The Sharp Edge approach from the north rivals Striding Edge on Helvellyn for drama. Five arms reach to the south, each named as a separate fell: Blease, Gategill, Hall's, Doddick, and Scales. Below is the small village of Threlkeld which once earned a living from several mines in the area, and the granite quarry to the south.

BORROWDALE
MAP REF: 80NY2414

Borrowdale is the dale stretching south from the head of Derwent Water to Seathwaite. Scenically it can claim to be the best valley in the Lake District, walled by high crags, with broadleaved woodlands which are wild with colour in spring and autumn, and with a River Derwent crystal clear to its pebbly bed. The B5289 from Keswick runs through most of its length. Lodore Falls (see page 107) are a feature on its east side, and near by is Shepherds Crag, a famous rock-climbing area. The river is bridged at the hamlet of Grange, once in the ownership of Furness Abbey, which had a home farm there.

The valley narrows through National Trust woodlands south of Grange, and on the east side a short track leads to the Bowder Stone, a large rock perched – apparently precariously – on a narrow base, another of those features not to be missed by the Victorians. Then on the west side is Castle Crag, a tree-clad cone of rock reached by quarry tracks. On its summit are the defensive ditches of a Romano-British fort. The valley opens to Rosthwaite, another hamlet, where a branch valley, Stonethwaite, joins from the south-east. Stonethwaite was the subject of a land ownership dispute between Furness and Fountains Abbeys. In 1304 Edward I confiscated it, and with true Yorkshire cunning Fountains offered the king 40 shillings for it and got it! At Seatoller the B5289 leaves Borrowdale to climb Honister Pass. Honister quarries once provided employment for Seatoller cottagers. From the settlement an unclassified road continues to the head of Borrowdale at Seathwaite, above which, as every schoolchild used to be told, is the wettest place in England. When it rains there it rains hard, with 131 inches (333cm) annual average. Seathwaite is the starting point for many fell ascents and rock climbing areas, particularly for the Scafells via Styhead Pass, and for Great Gable.

BOWFELL

MAP REF: 86NY2406

The best view of Bowfell (2960ft) is from the head of the Eskdale road where it appears as a great pyramid. If there is a hub to the splayed wheel spokes of the high central fells this is it. However, it properly belongs to Great Langdale; for this is its great western wall; and from Stool End, Langdale is the main approach for walkers by the ridge of The Band. The best fell view of it is from the well-worn walkers' track from Langdale to Esk Hause, where the cliffs of its northern end, Hanging Knotts, tower dramatically over the waters of Angle Tarn. The very popular rock climbers' crags, however, are on the Langdale side. The views from the summit are very extensive.

BOWNESS-ON-WINDERMERE

MAP REF: 94SD4096

Bowness is the older of the two towns of Windermere and Bowness, and dates from the 10th or 11th century, when the area was colonised by Vikings. A Nordic chief called Vinand named the lake after himself 'Vinand's Mere'.

St Martin's Church, Bowness, is the parish church of Windermere. The Bowness rectory, the oldest inhabited house in the area, was built in the 15th century. In 1480 the church was destroyed by fire and a new one was built. Its outstanding feature is the 15th-century stained glass in the east window, thought to have come from

▲ Brantwood's lakeside gardens are particularly lovely during the spring and early summer

Cartmel Priory (see page 29).

The famous round house on Belle Isle in the middle of the lake, opposite Bowness, was built in 1774.

The first public steamer on Windermere was launched in 1845. Two years later the railway reached Windermere and Windermere village itself then began to develop (see page 60). Bowness expanded rapidly to cater for the influx of tourists, and several of the older hotels were established. In 1869 H W Schneider settled at 'Belsfield' and initiated many improvements. Among them was the pier just below his house. He used to walk down each morning preceded by his butler carrying his breakfast on a silver tray; he then had breakfast on his steam launch *Esperance* while it took him to

Lakeside, where a special train (he owned the railway) took him to his office in Barrow.

His pier is now used by the Bowness Bay Boating Company for their public launch service. *Esperance* is now one of the fine working collections of historic Lake District craft in the Windermere Steamboat Museum.

Steamers operate daily to Lakeside and Ambleside and there are minibuses for touring the area. Boats of all sorts may be hired.

The whole of the Bowness area is geared to the visitor trade during the season, and most leisure activities are represented.

THE WINDERMERE STEAMERS

There has been a 'steamer' passenger service on Windermere since 1845 when the paddle-propelled *Lady of the Lake* began her maiden voyage for the Windermere Steam Yacht Company to the accompaniment of the band of the Kendal Cavalry. She was followed by a second vessel, *Lord of the Isles*.

In 1848 a rival company, the Windermere Iron Steamboat Company, was established and a year later launched *The Firefly* and later *The Dragonfly*. These were new, faster vessels and the competition between the two companies was intense. The vessels raced each other. Fares were slashed. Rival brass bands on the decks tried to outblow each other. Touting for custom on Bowness promenade was noisy, and holidaymakers were in danger

of being press-ganged. At last the two companies merged in 1858.

Since then a number of steamers passed through several hands until the Windermere Iron Steamboat Company took control from 1985. The refurbished *Swan*, the *Teal* and the *Tern* now run a regular service from their Lakeside base, carrying around half a million passengers annually. The *Swan* (560 passenger capacity) replaced an earlier *Swan* in 1938. The *Teal* (also 560) was launched in 1936, replacing an earlier vessel

which ran for 48 years. In 1956 Her Majesty the Queen and Prince Philip sailed from Ambleside to Bowness in her. A fourth vessel, the *Swift*, was laid up in 1981 and is now a floating exhibition centre.

The *Tern* (350 capacity) is the oldest vessel, launched in 1891. It has been estimated that she has sailed a million miles and carried 12 million passengers. She was refurbished, ready to continue service on her 100th birthday.

Smart steamers cross Windermere daily ▼

▲ The National Park visitor centre at Brockhole offers, among other things, croquet, putting, trails and picnicking facilities in the grounds

BRANTWOOD

MAP REF: 92NY3195

Brantwood, on the east side of Coniston Water, was the home of John Ruskin for the last 29 years of his life. First Slade Professor of Fine Art at Oxford, he had already reached the height of his fame as outspoken author, artist, lecturer and critic. His views offended many, but attracted ardent disciples. He was highly respected in the local community in which he took an interest. Brantwood is open to the public, and contains many of his drawings, paintings, and personal possessions. (See also Coniston, page 63.)

BROCKHOLE

MAP REF: 88NY3800

About half way between Windermere and Ambleside, between the A591 and the lake shore, is Brockhole, the National Park's visitor centre. The large country house was built for Henry Gaddum, a Manchester businessman, in 1899. It now houses displays, and there are regular lectures. The Lake District National Park includes the whole of the Lakeland – 880 square miles, and is the largest in England and Wales. The function of the visitor centre is to illustrate the aims of the National Park and what it has to offer. The gardens, which reach down to the lake shore, are preserved as in the original plan.

It might be considered that for a proper understanding and enjoyment of the Lake District a visit here is a priority.

BROTHERS WATER

MAP REF: 82NY4012

Brothers Water, at the northern foot of Kirkstone Pass, is one of the smallest of the 12 lakes. Old maps show it as 'Broad Water'. Wordsworth suggests that the name change followed a tragedy when two brothers sliding on its ice, fell through and were drowned.

BROUGHAM

MAP REF: 77NY5328

When the Romans occupied the area it was probable that westbound British roads, from what is now Northumberland and Yorkshire, crossed with a north-south road at what is now Brougham. In fact it is still in the locality of crossroads – the M6 and the A6 with the A66. The Romans defended it with a fort they named *Brocavum*, which held up to 1000 infantry and cavalry. Eight centuries later the Normans had need to hold the strategic position which had added significance in the light of boundary disputes with Scotland, and Gospatric, son of Orm, used stone from the remains of the Roman fort to build Brougham Castle. It came into the hands of the Clifford family in the 13th century, and the last Clifford, Lady Anne, died here in 1676, after which the castle fell into disrepair. However, there is much left to see and it is arguably the most evocative remnant of its period in the north-west. It is in the care of English Heritage.

Brougham Castle by the River Eamont. The substantial remains include the 13th-century keep and later buildings ranged round a courtyard ▼

▲ The buildings of Caldbeck's old corn mill have been converted into a complex of craft and gift shops, with a working waterwheel and a mining museum

the care of the National Trust and the National Park owns shore on the east side, securing pedestrian access all round. The hamlet consists of two hotels, a small chapel and little else.

CALDBECK

MAP REF: 75NY3239

Caldbeck is on the northern boundary of the National Park.

It was made famous by John Peel, the renowned huntsman, who was born at Park End, Caldbeck, in 1776, and buried in Caldbeck churchyard on 13 November 1854, after a hunting accident at Ruthwaite. His gravestone is decorated with hunting symbols.

The words of the song 'D'ye Ken John Peel', by which he is immortalised, were written by his friend John Woodcock Graves at his home in Caldbeck after a day's

BROUGHTON-IN-FURNESS

MAP REF: 91SD2187

Broughton is an interesting little market town lying close to where the beautiful River Duddon joins the sea. It is on the southern edge of the National Park at the crossroads of the A593/595.

It was first mentioned as 'Brocton', meaning 'settlement by the brook', in 1196. The present church dates from the 11th century with Saxon walls and a Norman archway. The splendid Broughton Tower and its dungeons – to the north end of the town – are all that remain of the old castle of the Broughtons who settled in the area in Anglo-Saxon times and continued to flourish under the Normans and Plantagenets. Easily accessible, there are several public footpaths that traverse the old castle grounds.

Broughton retains its character as a compact 18th-century market town.

BUTTERMERE

MAP REF: 78NY1716

In the early days of popular tourism connoisseurs of landscape had Buttermere at the top of the list. Nothing has changed. The setting of the beautiful mile-and-a-half long lake is idyllic. Behind it is the wall of High Crag, High Stile and Red Pike, all over 2400ft, and white water spills down their sides; Sour Milk Gill is well named. To the east towers Fleetwith Pike (2126ft) by the side of Honister Pass, and it is via Honister Pass from Borrowdale that the lake is approached; or by Newlands Pass from Keswick via Braithwaite. Both passes can be closed by snow. The lake and much surrounding land is in

A level footpath hugs the shores of Buttermere, providing a delightful circular walk of just under five miles with many excellent views ▼

28

▲ Castlerigg, one of Britain's most dramatically sited stone circles, is another of the many properties in the Lake District belonging to the National Trust

hunting in 1832. After the poem was first sung to its original tune at the Rising Sun Inn, such was the applause that Graves is reported to have said: 'By Jove, Peel, you'll be sung when we're both run to earth!'

However, it was not until William Metcalfe, the choirmaster of Carlisle Cathedral, put new music to it in 1869 that it became a national song.

There is a plaque now outside the house where Graves composed the song, and in 1939 a shelter was erected opposite the church as a memorial to Peel and Graves.

CARTMEL

MAP REF: 70NY3778

Cartmel is a very attractive village half a mile outside the National Park.

The village is well known for its priory, built in 1188, of which only the gatehouse and church remains. The rest was destroyed when the priory was dissolved in 1536-7. The church was restored in 1620 by George Preston of Holker Hall and became the parish church. As a result, Cartmel now has one of only four monastic churches in Cumbria (apart from Carlisle Cathedral) that remained in use as parish churches after the Dissolution; and it is the only one in the county – and one of very few in England – where the whole church was preserved.

One of the features of this church is the Harrington family tomb, with its effigies of Sir John Harrington (who died in 1347) and his wife, both literally 'lifting up their hearts'.

The beautiful 14th-century monastic gatehouse in the village square was used from 1624 to 1790

as a grammar school. It was acquired by the National Trust in 1946 and is now an art gallery and folk museum.

Cartmel Races are set in a beautiful parkland and attract the top jockeys. A fairground atmosphere with stalls and refreshments transforms the park on race days.

CASTLERIGG STONE CIRCLE

MAP REF: 80NY2923

Castlerigg Stone Circle is two miles east of Keswick, approached by unclassified roads south of the A66. It

was previously called 'the Druid circle' but this and other circles in the area are of Neolithic/Bronze Age date, aeons before the arrival of the Druids. Other, mainly lesser, circles are around the Lakeland fringe; what is unique about Castlerigg is its central position surrounded by high fells – Blencathra to the north, Helvellyn range on the skyline to the south-east; surely the most dramatic setting of any circle, and a gift for photographers. The circle is in fact slightly oval with an entrance on the north, and on the east side is an oblong 'chamber'.

LAKE DISTRICT NATIONAL PARK

When William Wordsworth wrote his famous *Guide to the Lakes* for the early tourists, he expressed a concern about some of the undesirable changes that were taking place, and hoped that people would show more care. 'In this wish', he wrote, 'the author will be joined by persons of pure taste throughout the whole island, who, by their visits (often repeated) to the Lakes in the North of England, testify that they deem the district a sort of national property, in which every man has a right and interest who has an eye to perceive and a heart to enjoy.'

It could be said that he invented National Parks. The first move to protect at least part of the Lake District came in 1895 with the

formation of the National Trust, the now well-established charity which seeks to acquire and preserve property of national importance. Some of its earliest purchases were by Derwent Water. Although National Parks were designated in other parts of the world from the end of the 19th century, Britain did not get its National Parks Act until 1949. The Lake District became the largest of the ten National Parks of England and Wales, with 880 square miles. The task of a Park Authority, with its planning powers, is to preserve its area's beauty, and to ensure that the public have the freedom to enjoy it.

Although the Lake District National Park is not wholly in public ownership, its largely unspoilt landscape is at last protected as a 'sort of national property'.

COCKERMOUTH

MAP REF: 72NY1230

Cockermouth is an ancient market town now bypassed by the A66 cross-Cumbria trunk road. It stands in attractive countryside on the fringe of the National Park, at a point where the River Cocker joins the River Derwent.

The Romans recognised its strategic importance and controlled its warlike Brigante tribes from here. The castle was built in the 12th century so that the English could protect the area from the marauding Scots – but Robert the Bruce destroyed part of it in 1315. In the Civil War it was held for Parliament despite a siege in 1648. The building then fell into decay and just one wing, rebuilt last century, is now used as a residence by the Wyndham family; another is an estate office.

▲ Now known as Wordsworth House, the poet's birthplace was built in 1745

After being granted its market charter in 1221, Cockermouth gradually developed in importance as a market town. In 1568 Mary Queen of Scots stayed here after her flight from the Battle of Langside. In the 17th century it was the chief commercial centre in the old county of Cumberland. Although considerably developed since then, it has retained much of its original character. A typical Cumbrian agricultural show is held here each summer, with classes for livestock, produce and crafts; also hound trails and Cumberland and Westmorland wrestling.

Some famous people have been born in Cockermouth or the surrounding villages. These include Fletcher Christian, the *Bounty* mutineer, who was born at Moorland Close and baptised at Brigham in 1764; John Dalton, the discoverer of the atomic theory, who was born in 1766 in Eaglesfield; and, of course, poet William Wordsworth, who was born in Cockermouth's Main Street in 1770. The house is now in the possession of the National Trust and open to the public (see page 63).

CONISTON AND CONISTON WATER

MAP REF: 92SD3097

Coniston village was born of the mining industry. Coniston Old Man, which towers behind, is riddled with old mine holes, now abandoned. By contrast, the scene in front, over Coniston Water, is relatively mild, consisting largely of the slopes of Grizedale Forest. The reason for the difference is that Coniston itself is on the edge of the craggy Borrowdale volcanic rocks, while to the east is the softer rock landscape of the Silurian slates. The rail link to Coniston was axed, sadly, as it was a beautiful scenic run.

Coniston Hall, by the lake side to the south of the village, is Coniston's oldest building, dating from the 16th century. It was the home of the Le Flemings, the largest landowners.

John Ruskin was the village's most famous resident (see Brantwood page 27). A little museum contains some of his studies and pictures, letters and photographs. Here also is his collection of geological specimens, and pictures by his talented secretary W Collingwood. The memorial cross which marks his grave in the local churchyard was designed by Collingwood.

In effect, Coniston Water is a public highway with launching at Coniston landings. Since the National Park Authority placed a 10 mph speed limit on the lake it is largely occupied by sail. However, there is a tangible reminder of the days when the Furness Railway Company ran a tourists' steamer service on the lake. One of the steamers was the *Gondola*, so named for its eccentric shape. Restored and rebuilt by the National Trust, the *Gondola* steams again, quietly around the lake for the enjoyment of a modern public.

The lake is five miles long and a little over 180ft deep at its deepest point. Most of the west shore is in the care of the National Trust and the National Park, and there is a great area of public access. A narrow road follows the eastern side.

The lake has been used on several occasions for attempts at the world water speed record. The last attempt was in 1967 when Donald Campbell was killed as he reached an estimated speed of 320 mph. The accident occurred over the deep water, and Campbell's body and most of the wreckage have not been recovered.

Campbell's memorial in Coniston. He was travelling at 320mph when he died ▼

CONISTON OLD MAN

MAP REF: 92SD2797

The Old Man of Coniston (2631ft) stands to the west of Coniston village. The mines no longer exist. The main activity was directly above the village by Church Beck, now known as Coppermines Valley. In the early days the copper ore was carted all the way to Keswick for smelting. Later it was carried down to Coniston Hall quay and taken down lake to Nibthwaite and then carted to Greenodd to be shipped to St Helens for smelting. The railway came to Coniston in 1859 at the height of mining activity. The decline in the industry came at the end of the century when there were cheaper imports.

Coniston Old Man is much favoured by fell walkers, the popular route being by the fell gate and Low Water, and the summit is frequently thronged. The more adventurous, however, explore the outlying arms of the sprawling Old Man range: Wetherlam, 2502ft, which dominates much of the viewpoint from the east, Swirl How, 2630ft, to the north and Grey Friar, 2536ft, on the north-west. The great 600ft-high wall of Dow Crag, overlooking Goats Water on the western side, was discovered by rock climbers in the early days of the

▲ Coniston Old Man from Brantwood on the eastern shore of Coniston Water

here that in 926 the 'Peace of Dacre' was signed by Athelstan of England and Constantine of Scotland. In the churchyard are four very old mysterious stones representing four bears: anti-clockwise – bear asleep leaning on staff, bear being attacked by cat, bear reaching to grab cat, bear eating cat. Their origin is unknown.

A short distance away by Dacre Beck is the medieval castle. Here again the castle is on the site of an earlier structure, but the present building dates from the 14th century. It was lost to the Dacre family after Leonard Dacre was involved in an ill-fated insurrection against Queen Elizabeth I. The castle was restored under the ownership of the·Earl of Sussex in 1675, and there was further work in 1789. The castle is open to the public only by written appointment.

sport, and still offers its challenge. South of the heights the once busy but rough Walna Scar road links Coniston with Dunnerdale. It is now a mere path.

CRUMMOCK WATER
MAP REF: 78NY1519

Crummock Water is twice the size of its neighbour, Buttermere, which feeds it, but has only half the beauty, lacking the drama of overlooking crags. Nevertheless, it has its attractions, best seen after a scramble up on to Rannerdale Knotts, above the road on its east side which follows most of its length. Like Buttermere, it can be circumnavigated on foot, though the way is rather rough.

DACRE
MAP REF: 76NY4526

Dacre village, north of Ullswater and west of the A592, is of great historical interest. The present church dates from Norman times and has features dating from the 12th and 13th centuries. There are carved stones, however, of much earlier origin, for the church stands on the site of a Saxon monastery (as recent excavations have proved). The monastery was mentioned by the Venerable Bede 'near the River Dacore' under the care of Abbot Swidbert, and later Thruidred. It was

DALEMAIN
MAP REF: 77NY4726

The large, pink limestone Georgian-fronted house of Dalemain can be seen from the A592 north of Ullswater. It is open to the public (see under Dacre, page 63). The house has been the ancestral home of the Hasells since 1665. The façade hides building dating back to a medieval defensive tower, and there are Elizabethan and Jacobean features. The house has a friendly, 'lived in' feeling. A barn holds old agricultural machinery, refreshments are served in the old hall, and there are fallow deer in the surrounding pleasant park land.

A lovely countryside park with fallow deer provides the setting for Dalemain. There are tours of the house, three museums to visit and rare plants in the gardens ▼

DERWENT WATER

MAP REF: 80NY2519

The best view of Derwent Water, the third largest lake and the favourite of many, is from Friar's Crag, south of the Keswick boat landings, where a long vista of the lake is seen framed in shaggy woodlands, and with the crags of Borrowdale in the distance. Here, it is said, monks and pilgrims would gather to be blessed by St Herbert, who had his hermitage on St Herbert's island in the centre of the lake. Bede records the close friendship between the hermit and St Cuthbert. The lake has three other islands, Derwent Isle, near Friar's Crag, Lord's Island, to the south, and Rampsholme, south of that.

Much of the surrounding land and the lake is in the care of the National Trust and it is possible to explore the delightfully wooded shores by using the scheduled motor boat service which has pick-up landing stages around the lake. Other viewpoints over the lake can be had from the high-level narrow road on the west side.

Friar's Crag: all four of the islands on Derwent Water are visible from here ▼

The lake is subject to a 10 mph speed limit which preserves an air of quietness. The shallower northern end of the lake freezes in hard winters making skating possible. Derwent Water, with Bassenthwaite Lake, is the home of a rare whitefish, the vendace (*Coregonus albula*).

DOVE COTTAGE
MAP REF: 87NY3406

Dove Cottage at Grasmere was called Town End cottage when William Wordsworth and his sister Dorothy moved there in 1799. Originally it was an inn called the Dove and Olive Branch. In the years to 1808 when the poet lived here, he wrote some of the most famous lines in the English language, including 'Intimations of Immortality', 'Resolution and Independence', 'The Brothers', 'Michael', 'The Recluse', and poems included in the *Lyrical Ballads* 1800 edition. In 1802 William brought his new wife here, childhood friend Mary Hutchinson, and when the family began to grow they were forced to leave for larger accommodation in Grasmere village. There were often guests at Dove Cottage, including Sir Walter Scott, and Wordsworth's great friend Coleridge had a house at Keswick, so there were frequent exchange visits. Dorothy Wordsworth's journal tells of those productive years at the cottage.

When the Wordsworths left, the tenancy was taken by Thomas De Quincey, who wrote *Confessions of an Opium Eater* and later *Recollections of the Lake Poets*.

The house is owned by a charitable trust and is open to the public. It remains largely as the Wordsworths knew it, and the garden is faithfully kept as the poet planned it. There is also a delightfully imaginative museum which has occasional special exhibitions, and an excellent book shop.

DUNNERDALE
MAP REF: 91SD2195

The Duddon valley was a favourite of Wordsworth and inspired *The River Duddon, a Series of Sonnets*. But Dunnerdale is the name given to the eight-miles-long valley of the River Duddon from Cockley Beck, between Wrynose and Hard Knott Passes, to Duddon Sands on the southern coast. At the head of the valley, south of Black Hall under Harter Fell, is the Forestry Commission's forest which raised bitter controversy when planting began in 1936. Now the forest has matured it is more acceptable. The Commission have made a car park near Hinning House

▲ The ruins of Egremont Castle stand in a park at the southern end of the town

which is a base for many walks in this lovely valley which only lacks a lake. Seathwaite-in-Dunnerdale has a little chapel, restored and 'improved' in Victorian times in spite of John Ruskin's protests. Here from 1736 was 'Wonderful Walker', the parson revered and praised by many for his industry. He was curate in charge for 66 years, starting with a stipend of £5 per annum. He worked on the surrounding farms, spun his own wool, and his wife made their clothes. He brewed and sold beer, taught the local children, wrote letters for the illiterate, gave to charity, raised and educated a family. When he died at the age of 92, in the same year as his wife, he left a fortune of £2,000 in his will.

Down valley is the hamlet of Ulpha. Ulpha is a Norse name meaning probably the 'hay' or park of Ulf, but some prefer the more romantic suggestion that its meaning is 'wolf hill', from 'ulf-hauga'. The road divides at Ulpha, the main way crossing a bridge and going on directly on the river's east bank to Duddon Bridge and the A595 and Broughton. The other way on the west bank is narrow and tortuous, joining the Thwaites Fell road before reaching Duddon Bridge, but passing on its way, just before the bridge, Duddon forge. The forge, erected in 1736 and worked until 1867, had great bellows worked by water power. Charcoal for the furnace was collected from woodland many miles around. The substantial remains are in the care of the National Park Authority, whose permission should be sought for access.

Below the bridge several ancient ways cross Duddon Sands which are in fact still classed as public roads. At low tides they were once important lines of communication for local people who were aware of the sand's dangers and knew where the changeable river's course could be

crossed. Now the ways are footpaths which still require that local know-how.

EGREMONT
MAP REF: 70NY0110

This old market town, with a wide tree-lined main street, developed where the west coast route (A595) crosses the Ehen River flowing from Ennerdale.

One of its attractions is the 12th-century Norman castle, built of Red Sandstone. It was destroyed in the 16th century and is now a ruin, but the gatehouse is still very impressive.

Also open to the public is the Lowes Court Gallery, a 16th-century building restored by local enthusiasts to promote appreciation of the arts. All work exhibited is by artists living in Cumbria or with strong local connections; there are regular exhibitions. There is a street market every Friday.

Egremont is famous for its Crab Fair. Held since 1267, this old-fashioned country fair is connected with fruit not fish, and is held in celebration of the crab apple. The parade of the Apple Cart takes place in the main street at 12.30pm on the third Saturday in September, when apples are thrown to the public.

The main street then also becomes the site of the 'greasy pole' competition, with the pole itself being erected at dawn on the day of the fair. This originally had a sheep fastened to the top – the prize for anyone able to scale the 30ft pole without artificial aids. These days the reward is in kind – and remember it's the glory not the reward that counts.

In the evening the World Gurning Championships are held. The person who can pull the most grotesque face through a horse collar is the winner.

There are also track and field events, shows and hound trails during the day.

▲ Peace and solitude are virtually guaranteed in the secluded valley of Ennerdale. The lake is accessible to pedestrians only

ELTERWATER
MAP REF: 87NY3304

Elter Water, at the foot of Great Langdale, is one of the smaller lakes, with a complicated shape and aggravatingly difficult to view. It takes all the flow of water from both Great and Little Langdale, the outflow being the River Brathay, which eventually pours over the falls below by Skelwith Bridge. 'Elter' is a Norse name for swan, so this is 'Lake of the Swans', particularly significant when the migrating whooper swans visit the lake in the winter.

Quarrying remains an industry for the area north of the lake, but Elterwater village was famous for its gunpowder works powered by six water wheels, in production from 1824 until after World War I. The site is now a holiday complex.

ENNERDALE
MAP REF: 78NY1015

The westernmost valley of the Lake District is less accessible than the other dales. The approach to Ennerdale Water is by a narrow road which ends at a Forestry Commission car park at Bowness Knott. The continuing private road by the lake's northern shore is a right of way for pedestrians. Ennerdale Water has its head in the fierce volcanic crags. On its southern side the great hump of Pillar (2927ft), with Pillar Rock – famous for its rock climbs – standing before it, hides a view of Great Gable behind. On Pillar's eastern side are Steeple (2760ft) and Haycock (2618ft). At the valley head is Black Sail Pass, with the district's remotest Youth Hostel. The fells on the northern head, which are the rear sides of the Buttermere crags, are largely hidden by the forestry.

The Forestry Commission acquired the land around the lake in 1926 and planting began a year later. Farming ceased at the head of the dale, and this, together with the fact that fell access for walkers and climbers could be affected, aroused controversy. The Commission has frequently met with criticism for the unnatural, straight-edged boundaries but nowadays is more enlightened and is making sensitive adjustments.

Ennerdale Water is a delight, and the fact that it is a reservoir serving West Cumbria is not at all obvious. It is possible to enjoy a quiet, though slightly rough, eight-mile walk all around the lake.

ESKDALE
MAP REF: 84NY1701

Boot village is regarded as the heart of Eskdale, but the River Esk rises six miles upwards by Esk Hause, the 2490ft-high crossroads of the fells, then is fed by the waters spilling from the eastern faces of the Scafells on to a wet, boulder-littered area more remote and wild than anywhere else in the Lake District, before reaching the green pastures of Brotherilkeld under Hard Knott Pass. It is then that the river makes its delectable way through the gentler contours of Eskdale by Boot. Above Brotherilkeld was once the sheep farm of Furness Abbey which was given licence by the Lord of Millom to enclose its holding, as long as the dyke was low enough to allow deer to cross.

The Romans had made their presence known below this area. Their road came by Hardknott Fort (see page 38), which overlooks the dale, and down by the Esk to their port and fort at Ravenglass. Only traces of the road can now be found.

At Boot there is a corn mill, carefully restored by the County Council and open to the public. There has been a mill in Eskdale certainly since medieval times, and probably before that. South of Boot is the wooded ravine of Stanley Gill, which holds the much visited waterfall in the care of the National Park Authority. Here, too, is Dalegarth Station, the terminus for the narrow-gauge Ravenglass and Eskdale Railway, commonly known as 'La'al Ratty'. There is a regular, very popular passenger service between here and Ravenglass (see page 52). During the season the carriages are hauled by handsome little steam engines. The line previously served mines, then quarries, in Eskdale, carrying their loads to the port and main railway line at Ravenglass.

The little, barn-like church of St Catherine at Boot stands in a perfect setting for worship, down by the River Esk. It is almost certain that Furness monks had their chapel here in the 14th century; but it is quite probable that the site's history goes farther back than that.

Down valley from Boot the road divides, the road to the right goes past the Outward Bound School to Eskdale Green and westwards. The narrow, leftward way goes south for Dunnerdale, but a narrow road turns

THE HILL FARMER

Hill farming has been practised in the Lake District for a thousand years. One reason that it survives today, in the modern, difficult economic climate, is that the farms are largely in the hands of families who have been in the business for many generations and know how to make the best of what they have. It is a way of life that they firmly defend. No financial speculator would consider buying into Lakeland hill farming. Most of the land, in farming terms, is very poor. Even the best land, the 'inby', close to the farm in the valley, falls far short of the quality expected by lowland farmers.

The fell farmer must work to a routine that has changed little over the centuries. Lambs are born to the hardy hill sheep from the middle of April. At the end of May they are put on the hills with the off it to continue with the meandering Esk to the A595. Beyond that the Esk curves round the edge of Muncaster Castle's land to the sea at Ravenglass.

ESTHWAITE WATER

MAP REF: 93SD3596

Between Windermere and Hawkshead is little Esthwaite Water, first beloved of Wordsworth when he was at school at Hawkshead. School started in the early morning, but the boy was up betimes:

> . . . My morning walks
> Were early; – oft before the
> hours of school
> I travelled round our little
> lake, five miles
> Of pleasant wandering.
> Happy time!
>
> *(The Prelude)*

Esthwaite is often first viewed after passing Far and Near Sawrey *en route* for Hawkshead from the Windermere ferry. The road skirts its eastern side and the Pikes of Langdale can be seen across its water. At the lake head is Priest Pot, a rare fen area gradually forming over accumulated silt protected as a National Nature Reserve. Being small, low lying, and surrounded by farmed land, the lake is rich in nutrients and supports some good fishing, notably for pike, and there is perch, rudd and roach, as well as trout. The lake is owned by Esthwaite Estates and boating permits (no powered boats) are available from the Trout Farm.

▲ Once great Furness Abbey

FURNESS ABBEY

MAP REF: 70SD1969

Down a by-road between Dalton and Barrow-in-Furness, in the care of English Heritage, are the very impressive remains of the second largest and most powerful abbey in the North of England – Furness Abbey. Its quiet position in 'The Vale of the Deadly Nightshade'; its Red Sandstone walls which glow as if red-hot in certain light effects, standing within a course or two to their original height in the transepts and choir; the elaborately fluted arches to the superb ruin of the chapter house; the soaring sides of the great east window; the western tower, also almost to original height – all give a tremendous impression.

Building of the abbey began in 1127 by the Savigny Order when it had been decided to transfer to this site from Tulketh, near Preston. They worked on the building for 20 years, then the Order merged with the Cistercians and the original church was enlarged and the ten-bay nave was built. The crossings were built and the usual period feature, a belfry tower was erected above it. In the 15th century an attempt to heighten this tower apparently resulted in a collapse and the western tower was constructed as a result.

The chapter house is entered through a vaulted vestibule. Only portions remain but the beauty of the arched windows, and the remains of the slender columns have an impressive effect. Viewed from the cloister square the five decorated arches to chapter house, parlour and slype make a perfect picture. South of the arches are the remains of the 12-bay undercroft, the largest in England, which had above it the monks' dormitory. The great size testifies to the abbey's importance. Little remains of the quarters of the lay brothers at the opposite side of the cloister.

Of the great 14th-century infirmary there is little trace, but the chapel, with its vaulted roof, still stands. The scattered lay-out of the establishment can be seen, with the usual cunning arrangement of water courses. Some boundary walls can be traced. The whole of this main site was once walled, enclosing some 22 acres.

There is a useful little visitor centre which explains the fascinating history of the place with enlarged displays of original documents and manuscripts.

ewes. Haymaking, sheep dipping and clipping follow, and the sales are in the autumn. The survival of the tough little Lakeland Herdwick breed, that can live out the winter on high land, is due largely to the supportive conservation policy of the National Trust, which owns many of the farms.

Faced with the uncompromising reality of the mountainous terrain, the hill farmer has to cooperate, rather than contend, with nature. The unique quality of the Lakeland landscape is due largely to the harmonious working relationship that the hill farmer has always had with his land. The future of hill farming depends not only on European economic policies, but also on our own attitude to the continuing care of the countryside.

Herdwick, one of the hardiest breeds, has been in the Lake District for almost 1000 years. Its thick fleece was made into 'hodden grey' cloth ▶

GOSFORTH

MAP REF: 70NY0603

This large village, now almost a small town, lies on the western boundary of the National Park.

It is notable for the ancient 10th-century cross in the churchyard, which is of national importance. Fourteen feet high, complete and remarkably slender, the cross has pagan and Norse devices on one side and Christian symbols on the other. Both tell the story of the triumph of good over evil. The Christian interpretation of a Norse legend is believed to be indicative of the transition from pagan beliefs to Christianity, although at the time the very survival of Christianity was in doubt.

GRANGE-OVER-SANDS

MAP REF: 70SD4077

Grange-over-Sands, on the north shore of Morecambe Bay, has been called the Riviera of Cumbria. It lies on the B5277 which leaves the A590 midway between Levens and Newby Bridge.

Grange is a quiet, restful resort in a natural sun trap between the Lake District Fells and the sea. It is reputed to have a higher temperature in spring than any other place in the north of England.

The coming of the railway in 1857 made Grange one of the most popular holiday resorts for Lancashire folk at a time when the Furness area was part of Lancashire.

Now it is part of Cumbria, but the old connection between Furness and Lancashire is still evident in its 'over-Sands' title. For it was the route over the sands of Morecambe Bay that linked the two parts of Lancashire before the railway. Even the Romans used this route. Then it became the short cut for the monks of Furness Abbey to get to and from Lancaster, and later a stage coach route.

However, the sands were always tricky, and as far back as the 16th century the Duchy of Lancaster appointed an official guide to lead people across the sands and gave him rent-free use of a house in Grange.

Behind Grange is Hampsfell, the summit of which (where there is an old shelter for 'wanderers') offers marvellous views on a clear day of the Isle of Man, the Yorkshire hills and the Lake District Fells. There is a Nature Trail through deciduous woodlands and open limestone fells

Gardens with tropical trees, an ornamental lake and a promenade lined with flower gardens contribute to the charm of Grange-over-Sands ▶

to the summit, and a leaflet about this is available at the Tourist Information Centre. Fishing permits may also be obtained there.

GRASMERE

MAP REF: 87NY3307

Grasmere is the northernmost village in the southern Lake District, set in a valley surrounded by hills. It lies two and a half miles south of the watershed at Dunmail Raise. The main settlement is a quarter of a mile north of Grasmere Lake.

The church in the village centre is dedicated to St Oswald, the oldest part being said to date from the 13th century. Grasmere's most famous resident, the poet Wordsworth, who lived in the village from 1799 to 1813, described the church (in *The Excursion*) as a building of 'rude and antique majesty', with 'pillars crowded' and 'naked rafters intricately crossed'.

From 1799 to 1808 Wordsworth lived at Dove Cottage (see page 33), about a quarter of a mile from the village, just off the main road. In 1808 the Wordsworth family moved to Allan Bank, a house now owned by the National Trust on the north side of Grasmere, but not open to the public. Later (1811) the Wordsworth family moved to the Rectory. Then they went to live in Rydal (see page 52). William and his wife, as well as his sister Dorothy and other members of his family, are buried in Grasmere churchyard.

Wordsworth taught in a tiny schoolroom built by public subscription in 1687. This is now the famous Gingerbread shop, situated near the church.

The annual Rushbearing Festival is held on the Saturday nearest 5 August. Children carrying bearings of flowers and rushes in traditional patterns follow the band through the village; then the bearings are placed in the church to commemorate the time when rushes constituted the flooring of the church. The famous Grasmere Sports are held on the Thursday nearest 20 August and include local sports such as Cumberland and Westmorland wrestling, fell races, and hound trailing.

▲ Grasmere Lake, with Rydal Water beyond, seen from Silver Howe. This is Wordsworth country, and the footpaths beside the lakes and on the surrounding fells were much loved and often walked by the poet and his family

Grasmere is a good centre for many fell walks and climbs. There is a National Park Information Centre (see page 65).

GREAT GABLE

MAP REF: 85NY2110

Great Gable falls a little short of the 3000ft mountains by 51 feet, but it remains as popular with fell walkers and rock climbers as its four larger rivals (the two Scafells, Helvellyn and Skiddaw). Its high hulk can be seen from so many viewpoints throughout Lakeland: as a great gable-end from Wasdale Head; and from east and west like a huge blunted stump. It really belongs to Wasdale, but it is separated from Scafell and Scafell Pike by the curving high valley which holds Lingmell Beck, and the Wasdale-Borrowdale walkers' route over Sty Head Pass.

There are several well-used ways to its summit. From Wasdale Head a path goes by its western flank to Beck Head, and then direct to the summit; from Borrowdale the route is taken to Sty Head Pass, and the top is reached north-west from there; from Honister Pass a quarry track rises, from whence a route can be taken by Gillercombe, Gable's neighbour,

Green Gable, and across the well-named Windy Gap.

Rock climbers contour westwards from Sty Head on the interesting Girdle Traverse to Great Napes, and some of the best climbs in the area – indeed where the sport of climbing really began last century. The climbs were named by those early pioneers: Tophet Bastion, Needle Ridge, Eagle's Nest Ridge, Arrow Head; and near the centre is the famous slender spire of

rock, Napes Needle, first climbed in 1886 by the legendary Walter Parry Haskett-Smith. He climbed it again 50 years later at the age of 74!

The summit is a confused mass of broken rock. It bears a bronze tablet which records the gift of the fell by the Fell and Rock Climbing Club to the National Trust as a war memorial to its colleagues. A well-attended service is held here every Remembrance Sunday at the 11th hour.

GRIZEDALE FOREST

MAP REF: 93SD3394

In 1936 the Forestry Commission acquired the estate in the ownership of Grizedale Hall. This now is Grizedale Forest, extending to over 4200 acres between Hawkshead and Esthwaite to the east side of Coniston Water. The hall, being too expensive to maintain, was regretfully demolished after serving, during the last war, as a prisoner-of-war camp for German officers.

Grizedale was the first of the Commission's forests to encourage recreational access by the public. It is now a major recreational resource, with waymarked routes for walkers, a cycle route, car parks and picnic sites. By the forest offices, housed in outbuildings once belonging to the hall, there is a visitor centre, a shop, and a childrens' playground. Here also is the now renowned 'Theatre in the Forest', founded by the Grizedale Society in the late 1960s, where musicians of national and international note are regularly featured.

In 1977 the Grizedale Society launched a scheme to encourage sculptors to use the forest as a working environment. With the encouragement of Northern Arts this has continued and it is possible to walk around the forest and to see examples of some of the work. A redundant saw mill has also been adapted to provide the 'Gallery in the Forest, and Crafts Workshop'. There are regular exhibitions.

Although most of the forest has been planted with conifers, there are still the remains of ancient broadleaved forest, and plenty of variety in the scene, and an abundance of wildlife. One of the virtues of a forest for recreation is the sense of remoteness, no matter how populated. Crowds vanish among the trees. A walk in the forest, at any time of year in any weather, can be most rewarding.

◄ The Forestry Commission has provided nature trails, waymarked walks and picnic sites in Grizedale Forest

▲ The Romans built *Mediobogdum*, their fort known as Hardknott Castle, to defend the road linking Ambleside and Ravenglass

HARD KNOTT
MAP REF: 85NY2301

Hard Knott Pass, rising to 1291ft, is well known for being the most difficult road in England – narrow, with hairpin bends and inclines of up to one-in-three (and quickly blocked at holiday weekends). The road follows the old Roman link road, the tenth iter, from Ambleside fort via Wrynose Pass to Ravenglass fort and port. The pass rises from Cockley Beck on the east and descends to the head of the Eskdale road near Brotherilkeld on the west.

To defend their road the Romans built their fort, *Mediobogdum,* on a shelf on the Eskdale side of Hard Knott. Although much of the stone was removed over the centuries, the wall remnants (375 feet square) and the foundations of the buildings are still impressive. But the site itself is extraordinary. There is a tremendous view of Eskdale to the sea; on a clear day the Isle of Man is visible; and to the north is the Scafell range. The site looks even more dramatic in foul weather. The land on three sides of the fort falls away rapidly, on the north and west almost sheer. The only way open to attack was from the pass summit, and on this side of the fort a deep trench was dug. The fort interior follows the standard pattern with a tower at each corner and a gate in each wall, with the granary and the headquarters buildings in the centre. Between the fort and the road can be seen the remains of the bath house. Above the fort, to the east, a parade ground has been levelled out of the fell side – an extraordinary piece of engineering.

Part of an inscription has been found on a stone which was originally over the main gate. It records that the fort was built (or rebuilt?) by a cohort from Dalmatia (modern-day Yugoslavia) for the 'Emperor Caesar Trajan Hadrian Augustus'. Pottery finds suggest that the fort was occupied between AD120 and 197.

HAVERTHWAITE
MAP REF: 93SD3483

Haverthwaite lies on the north bank of the River Leven. The village is mainly contained between the main road (A590) and the river which flows out of Windermere; but the Haverthwaite base of the Lakeside and Haverthwaite Railway – for which Haverthwaite is becoming increasingly well known and popular – is on the north side of the main road.

Getting up a good head of steam at Haverthwaite station ▼

The steam engines and carriages are kept in sheds and sidings at Haverthwaite. There are always engines to be seen, often from the main road, and with steam up; there is a big car park by the sheds. A daily train service operates between Haverthwaite, Newby Bridge and Lakeside from May to the end of October, with some running at other times (tel. 05395 31594).

HAWESWATER
MAP REF: 83NY4713

Last century the Haweswater valley was a place of dairy farms. The village of Mardale stood at its head, and the area was much praised for its beauty. But Manchester Corporation acquired the area, for the demands of the busy industrial areas around Manchester could not be met by Thirlmere's water, and a raised Haweswater would fill the need. In 1929 the corporation began to build the dam. Mardale and its farms, and its pub, the Dun Bull, were eventually drowned. Conifer trees were planted and the valley was completely changed. Now only the dam (not all that visible from most viewpoints) and the shore bleach marks left by the fluctuating levels of the enlarged lake, betray the fact that it is a reservoir. There is no denying that the Haweswater area has its attractions. The golden eagles consider this so. They have come to this valley after an absence of two centuries and with the cooperation of North West Water, the Royal Society for the Protection of Birds has the nest sites in its care.

The valley is walled on its west side with the long fell of High Street range (2719ft).

HAWKSHEAD

MAP REF: 87SD3598

Once all roads led to Hawkshead. It was an important market town used by Furness Abbey, which owned the land here from Windermere to Coniston. Wool was the wealth. The settlement's influence declined after the Dissolution, and even more, early last century, when Ulverston's market was a greater attraction. The oldest

▲ Red Tarn, lying below Helvellyn's dramatic Striding Edge

▲ Hawkshead Courthouse formed part of the manorial buildings held by Furness Abbey

building is the 500-years-old Court House, the abbey's only remaining manorial building. The village itself has picturesque 17th-century timbered buildings around alleyways and the square. The old Grammar School, where William Wordsworth was schooled, remains protected and open to the public. Anne Tyson's cottage, where the scholar lodged, is also unchanged; though if he stayed here at all it was only for a short time, for the Tysons moved to Colthouse on the village fringe, and it is this lodging that is referred to in *The Prelude*.

The church dates from the 15th century, but an earlier church also stood here. Inside there are decorations and painted texts dating from 1680. One of the little shops has been opened by the National Trust as an award-winning Beatrix Potter gallery, with some of the author/artist's original drawings and illustrations on display. Beatrix Potter gave much of the local property to the Trust (see also Near Sawrey, page 49).

HELVELLYN

MAP REF: 81NY3415

The constant stream of walkers up Helvellyn is evidence of the fell's prime popularity. It is accessible from both its west and east flanks, and it is one of the four fells over 3000ft (3116). The east side is quite dramatically different from the west, for it was here that the ice of the Ice Age, away from the milder west

winds, survived the longest, to leave hollow coves. The west side curves down to the Thirlmere valley, and from this side there are two well-known routes: one begins from the little chapel of Wythburn (all that remains of Wythburn village when the lake level was raised); and another runs from the car park provided by North West Water to the north at Swirls. The east side offers the more dramatic approaches. The path above the Grisedale valley leads to Striding Edge, a narrow *arête* separating the depths of Nethermost Cove from those containing Red Tarn. At the other end of the Red Tarn cove is another, less striking *arête*, Swirral Edge, often used as a descent route on the round walk. The range sprawls some six miles, south to north, with a number of summits: Dollywaggon Pike, Nethermost Pike, Low Man, Raise, Stybarrow Dod and Great Dod.

The summit is crowned with a cross shelter wind-break, and there is a memorial, with quotes from Wordsworth and Sir Walter Scott, to the dog which stayed faithfully by its master's side for three months when he died. The views are, of course, extensive, taking in most of the high fells and across to the Pennines in the east. Snow lingers on the east side well into spring, and walkers early in the season should first enquire about conditions from National Park information centres.

▲ Hesket Newmarket's wide main street and large green are typical of many northern towns. Several handsome 18th-century houses are to be seen here

HESKET NEWMARKET
MAP REF: 75NY3338

Before the 18th century Hesket (as it was then called) was probably only a small cluster of buildings, subsidiary to Caldbeck. Then, its most notable feature was Hesket Hall, built after 1630 for Sir Wilfred Lawson. This rather curious square building has gabled wings, a pyramid roof and big central chimney.

During the early 18th century Hesket was granted a market charter and by 1751 it lengthened its name to Hesket Newmarket. As with other planned market towns, tight rules controlled the shape of the market place and the building frontage, with traders' houses looking on to a market cross, a coaching house and an inn.

HIGH STREET
MAP REF: 88NY4411

High Street is the long easternmost fell range, about nine miles long, between Haweswater and the fells of Martindale Common above Ullswater. Its highest point is 2719ft. What is remarkable about the fell is that a Roman road ran along its heights; probably linking the fort at Brougham with the one at Ambleside. It was almost certainly a Roman improvement of an ancient British route, chosen to be above the complex terrain with swamps and forest which were then at the lower levels. The eastern face is broken by fierce crags and in its coves there are two tarns, the very deep Blea Water, and Small Water. South of the

summit are peaks which show up prominently from many viewpoints: from north to south, Thornthwaite Crag, Froswick, Ill Bell and Yoke.

The summit plateau is grassy and even, and until the 19th century was the venue for the area's 'shepherds' meets', when shepherds would bring in their strays to be claimed. It was an excuse for revelry. Casks of beer were brought up, and the sports enjoyed even included horse racing. The summit is still named Racecourse Hill.

▲ Gleaming exhibits in the Motor Museum at Holker Hall

Holker Hall clock-house courtyard where refreshments are available ▼

HOLKER HALL
MAP REF: 71SD3577

Near Cark, by the B5278 road between Grange-over-Sands and Haverthwaite, is the outstanding 'stately home' of Holker Hall, home of the Cavendish family. The site was acquired from Cartmel Priory after the Dissolution by the Preston family, and the present building was begun in the early 17th century.

The homely atmosphere of the house is delightful. There are examples of classical furniture and paintings in every beautifully decorated room.

The gardens are matchless and there are some unusual tree specimens including one of the oldest Chile pines (monkey puzzle tree) in the country. It was blown over in the 1890s, hauled upright with chains and seven carthorses, and replanted. There are red deer and fallow deer in the grounds. In an outbuilding there is a motor museum.

HONISTER PASS
MAP REF: 79NY2213

Honister Pass (1176ft) links Borrowdale with Buttermere. Its quarry has long provided high-grade hard slate. The fell above the quarry is Fleetwith Pike (2126ft), and to the south is the southern end of the Derwent Fells, Dale Head (2473ft). The quarrying on Honister has provided high-quality slate for two centuries. Incredibly, early last century, before the internal road systems were improved, the slate was pack-horsed by fell paths via Wasdale Head to the port of Ravenglass.

IRTON CROSS

MAP REF: 84SD0900

Irton Church is reached from an unclassified road south-west of Santon Bridge. The churchyard offers a fine view of the fells to the west; but the great interest here is an Anglian cross, in excellent condition, which is well over 1000 years old. (A cross in a corner is a modern copy.) The cross has the intricate decoration of the period; complicated knot work and interlacing. A runic inscription has weathered away.

The intricately carved Anglian cross in Irton churchyard ▼

KENDAL

MAP REF: 95SD5192

The 'Auld Grey Town' of Kendal, on the old A66 south - north road, with a population of above 25,000, was the largest town in the old county of Westmorland.

The Romans first realised its strategic importance and built their fort *Alauna* in a crook of the River Kent, south of the present town. There was a Saxon settlement, (a 9th-century cross can be seen in the parish church), and then the Normans came in the 11th century and built a motte-and-bailey fortification on the west side of the town, of which the remains can be seen (now Castle Howe, surmounted by an 18th-century obelisk dedicated to liberty). In the 13th century the motte-and-bailey was abandoned and a stone castle was built on the east side of the River Kent, the ruin of which is a prominent feature.

The parish church, built in the 13th century on the site of an earlier one, is one of the largest in England, with five aisles. It has an 80ft tower and a peal of ten bells. The sword and helmet left behind by 'Robin the Devil' of Crook (see page 60) are on display. The church stands at the southern end of the town, now known as Kirkland.

The Castle Dairy in Wildman Street, as its name implies, once served the castle, at the time when Katherine Parr lived there. It is the oldest habitable stone-built house in the area and has many interesting period features, including carved oak beams and a hand-carved four-poster bed.

There was a thriving wool trade in the Kendal area by the 13th century. This was stimulated in 1331 when Edward III granted a special Letter of Protection to John Kempe of Flanders and Flemish weavers came to settle. They made Kendal England's pioneer wool town, and Kendal bowmen made 'Kendal Green' cloth famous throughout the land. Shakespeare refers to men wearing 'Kendal-green' in *Henry IV* Part I. Kendal's motto is *'Pannus mihi Panis'* (Wool is my bread).

Other trades and industries established themselves, many of them making use of the 'yards' off the main street.

Much of the industrial and social life of the time is reflected in the Museum of Lakeland Life and Industry which is housed in part of the Abbot Hall complex. Here you can also enjoy the Abbot Hall Art Gallery with its splendid collection of furniture, *objets d'art* and paintings, including many by the local artist George Romney. There are often special displays. Abbot Hall, built in 1759, is found next to the parish church.

Another museum well worth visiting is Kendal Museum of Natural History and Archaeology near the station. A 'Walk Through South Lakeland' series of dioramas depicts the natural history and geology of the area, while a fascinating array of objects of many kinds traces the human story.

There are two Kendal Town Trails, details of which may be obtained from the tourist office in the Town Hall. There is also a leaflet about the Serpentine Woods Nature Trail.

Entertainment is offered at the Brewery Arts Centre, with car park, on the main road not far from Abbot Hall. The Centre is open throughout the year with a photographic gallery, small theatre, exhibitions and changing events (tel. 0539 752133).

On the A65 (Lound Road) is the South Lakeland Leisure Centre. A wide variety of leisure and sports activities is available, including swimming; in the evening there are concerts and shows (tel. 0539 729777).

The Kendal Gathering is held in late August. This is a festival of varied first class entertainment, outdoor and indoor, ending with a torchlight procession.

The Westmorland County Show is held on the second Thursday in September. This features agricultural exhibitions of all kinds, crafts and farm produce as well as show jumping, Cumberland and Westmorland wrestling, carriage driving and dog shows.

Abbot Hall, in Kendal, housing Gillow furniture, paintings and *objets d'art* ▼

▲ The bedroom in the Museum of Lakeland Life, housed in Abbot Hall's stables

Kendal is famous for its Kendal Mint Cake, a hard, mint-flavoured sugar slab used on expeditions (including Everest) and sold in large quantities to visitors as well as walkers and climbers.

KENTMERE

MAP REF: 88NY4504

Kentmere is a small, scattered village at the head of Kentdale, four miles from Staveley, along a narrow winding road with pleasant views of meadows, woods and hills.

The church in Kentmere, St Cuthbert's, has 16th-century roof beams. Kentmere Hall, on the west side of the valley, has a 14th-century pele tower.

In the church is a bronze memorial to Bernard Gilpin, who was born at Kentmere Hall in 1517 and went on to become Archdeacon of Durham

Part of the kitchen in the Museum of Lakeland Life, Kendal ▼

and a leader of the Reformation. He was known as 'The Apostle of the North', and for his attacks on the Roman Church was in danger of being burnt at the stake in 1558. He was on his way to face charges of heresy when he had the good fortune to break his leg. Catholic Queen Mary died before he recovered and the Protestant Queen Elizabeth I restored him to his position as Archdeacon.

The public road ends in the village, where there is a small car park. From there footpaths wind westward to Troutbeck, eastward to Longsleddale, southward to Ings and northward to Kentmere reservoir. This was created by damming the streams which formed the headwaters of the Kent immediately below Kentmere Common. The water was used to supply the valley mills.

▲ A Cumbrian style farmhouse tea may include such delicacies as Layered Cumbrian Lamb with Herbs

LAKELAND FARE

Like so many traditional dishes, some Lakeland recipes originated in seasonal needs and the availability of ingredients. 'Easter ledges' is no longer on the dinner table but in the old days it was a healthy break from the winter diet of mutton and oatmeal. The dish consisted mainly of the leaves of 'ledges' or 'ledgers' (bistort), the new shoots of nettles, and blackcurrant or raspberry leaves, chives, and barley. All were boiled in a bag in the same pan as the meat. Butter, beaten egg and seasoning were then added when it was served.

In the 18th century rum was available, probably cheaply (or was it sometimes smuggled?) because of trading from the west Cumberland ports with the West Indies. Hence the making of 'rum butter'. It is still popular and is

served in some guest houses and cafés. It is made from the local butter, brown sugar, rum and nutmeg. Served on scones still warm from the oven, it is ambrosia!

Cumberland sausage is made in long un-linked lengths. Alas, some pretentious mysteries masquerade under the name; the genuine article is made from high pork content and secret spice ingredients. Some local butchers have mastered the secret, but it is now almost a tradition that the best sausage comes from Waberthwaite, south-east of Ravenglass.

The true local gingerbread also has a secret recipe. Gingerbread has long been sold in the little building near Grasmere Church which was once the village school.

◄ One of the eight main teams out on a training exercise. These, and the back-up teams, are run voluntarily

THE MOUNTAIN RESCUE TEAMS

With the tremendous increase in the number of people enjoying hill walking and climbing, it is inevitable that some have accidents and some get lost. It is the job of the volunteers of the Lake District's mountain rescue teams to aid people who find themselves in trouble. Their services are called upon well over 200 times a year.

Because of the complicated terrain – the valleys radiating from a central hub with no direct communication between each – it needs eight main teams to cover the high fells, with five others to provide active back-up and to deal with incidents on the periphery. There is also a team of specialists to help with accidents in old mines; and in mountain searches there is a team of Search and Rescue dogs and handlers. In serious incidents it is possible also to call upon the help of the RAF rescue helicopters. The service has the support of the police force, who are responsible for the call-out.

Nowadays the teams have the help of sophisticated equipment; but most of the money to purchase it is raised by public subscription and their members' own efforts.

Mountain rescue is not a glamorous job. The team members are hardly in search of fame. They are themselves mountaineers who have a concern for those like-minded enthusiasts who are in trouble. It is hard, and sometimes risky, work. Very often the rescue is in the teeth of storm, and often at night.

KESWICK

MAP REF: 80NY2623

Keswick could be the capital of northern Lake District. Once a busy mining centre, it is now almost solely dependent on tourism. With mountains and lakes in close proximity, it is a natural centre for walkers, climbers and tourists.

Sporadic mining gave way to more intensive activity in the area in the 16th century when the Company of Mines Royal, founded by an agreement between Queen Elizabeth I and businesses with mining interests, was empowered to 'search, dig, try, roast and melt all manners of mines and ores'. In 1565 50 German miners were brought to Keswick and made their home and headquarters on Derwent Island. There were about a score or more of productive mines, some of them quite rich. Keswick became the smelting centre of Lakeland. Six were in full production in the later part of the 16th century. Vast quantities of charcoal were required and woods around the whole of the north-west were, at one time, devastated. The activity declined from the 18th century; but an unusual rich mine in Borrowdale continued into the 19th. This was the 'wad', plumbago, or black lead mine. The mineral was so valuable it was protected by an armed guard. One industry that the mine produced was the making of lead pencils. There is still a pencil mill in Keswick, though black lead is now imported. The high quality products are in great demand by artists. The mill has a surprisingly fascinating museum.

Tourism began in Keswick from the mid-18th century following glowing accounts of the area from several notable writers. Coleridge rented Greta Hall (now part of a school) in 1800, and was later joined by his brother-in-law, Southey, who spent the rest of his life there. But tourism received its great boost from 1865 when the railway came to Keswick, and the town's substantial Victorian architecture is a result.

A two-week religious festival in July has now become a notable tradition.

The oldest building in Keswick is Crosthwaite Church, on the west side

◄ Keswick's boat landings on Derwent Water. The lake is about a 20-minute walk from the town centre

of the town. It is dedicated to St Kentigern, 7th-century missionary and Glasgow's patron saint, who is said to have preached here in 'the place of the cross'. Part of the church fabric dates from the 12th century; but one of the main interests is a marble memorial to Poet Laureate Robert Southey, with an epitaph composed by his friend Wordsworth.

The little, but charming museum in Station Road has specimens of the many minerals found in the area, and the large bizarre xylophone made from 'musical stones'. Keswick is the home of the Century Theatre which offers plays nightly in the season.

The centre of much activity of course is at the boat landings on Derwent Water, where the round-the-lake launch service and boat hire are available.

KIRKSTONE PASS
MAP REF: 88NY4008

Kirkstone Pass at 1489ft is the highest road pass in the Lake District. It was once considered a formidable obstacle, but the modern vehicle should make little of it. The severest incline is on the approach from Ambleside up 'The Struggle', where in old times passengers had to leave the coach to give the horses a chance – but then suffered the fright of a rapid descent when the coachmen liked to show off their skills. The pass is named from a large boulder which from certain angles, particularly when partly shrouded in mist, resembles a little chapel. The descent northwards is to Brothers Water; southwards to Windermere it offers a wide prospect over the Troutbeck valley.

LAKESIDE
MAP REF: 93SD3787

Lakeside is at the foot of Windermere. This was a Furness Railway terminus from 1869, and the steamer pier, already in passenger use, gave added service as a goods collection point for deliveries to the properties around the lake. The railway company expanded the existing tourist trade by placing their own steamers on the lake. Sadly, British Rail closed the branch line in 1965. A short three-mile length of line from Haverthwaite, however, was acquired by the Lakeside and Haverthwaite Railway Company, which runs a regular steam train service to link up with the steamers through the holiday season.

Loughrigg Tarn and the outline of Langdale Pikes. Most expert rock climbers have scaled these crags ▶

LANGDALE
MAP REF: 86NY3006

There are two Langdales – Great and Little. Great Langdale is probably the most frequented valley in the Lake District, as it is a main base for fell walkers and rock climbers. The famous Langdale Pikes are one of the most distinctive features of the Lake District: the two humps of Harrison Stickle (2415ft) and Pike o'Stickle (2323ft) are part of the stirring background scene from the head of Windermere, from across Esthwaite Water, from Tarn Hows, or from Loughrigg Tarn. Raven Crag and Gimmer Crag, on their southern faces, are the famous rock-climbing crags, as is the sheer face of Pavey Ark (2288ft) – another, less prominent of the Pikes, which is a magnificent backdrop to Stickle Tarn, sitting in a hollow 1500ft atop one of the most heavily used footpaths in the Lake District.

There are popular walking areas all around. At the head of Great Langdale is Bowfell (2960ft) and to the south is the spikey crest of Crinkle Crags. There are exciting routes over to Grasmere, along the pack-pony route to Borrowdale, or by Esk Hause to the Scafells.

At the foot of the Pikes is the deep ravine of Dungeon Ghyll, the waterfall which was one of the thrills on the Victorian tourists' itinerary.

On the side of Pike o'Stickle was the area's earliest industry. A vein of very hard volcanic rock was exploited here by Neolithic craftsmen. When struck the rock flakes in a similar way to flint. Stone axes were made here and traded throughout the British Isles.

They can be seen in many museums.

Much of the valley head, and the farms, are in the care of the National Trust.

The only settlement in the valley is at Chapel Stile, which once housed the employees of the Elterwater Gunpowder works and the local quarries. The valley's church is here – a 19th-century building which replaced a poor earlier chapel, where the curate, it is recorded, had to sell ale to support himself and his family.

The road up Great Langdale turns and narrows (for stretches to a single lane) beyond the Dungeon Ghyll hotels, and makes an ascent to go by Blea Tarn to Little Langdale. Blea Tarn was the scene of 'The Solitary' in Wordsworth's *The Excursion*.

However, Little Langdale, a more or less parallel valley to the south, is usually approached from the A593 Coniston Road by traffic bound for Wrynose Pass at the head of the valley. Little Langdale is tighter, and less accessible than Great Langdale. As it rises to Wrynose, traces of the Roman road, the tenth iter, from Ambleside fort to Hardknott and Ravenglass, can be seen on the hillside to the modern road's right.

On the southern side of the valley the steep fell is the end of Wetherlam, a northern sprawl of the Coniston Old Man range.

The village of Little Langdale can be passed through in a moment – just a few houses and a pub. To the south a lane leads to a ford, a hazard not to be recommended. A footpath, though, goes over a photogenic stone bridge, 'Slater Bridge', to a much quarried area and a route to High Tilberthwaite.

45

LEVENS HALL

MAP REF: 95SD4984

By the junction of the A590 and the A6 roads south of Kendal is Levens Hall. Its great interest is in its historic garden, laid out by Monsieur Beaumont, gardener to many of the great landowners of the day, who chose to spend the last 40 years of his life, to 1730, here. The garden has yew trees clipped to strange topiary shapes, the meaning of which, if any, is lost in time. The house is mainly Elizabethan, but the oldest part is the 14th-century defensive pele tower. Home of the Bagot family, it contains Italian plasterwork, Cardova leather wall-coverings, beautiful paintings, Cromwellian armour and Jacobean furniture. There is a fine collection of working model steam engines. Weather permitting, traction engines are in steam on Sundays.

(See page 63.)

▲ Big Bertha is one of the traction engines from the exhibition of working steam vehicles housed in an outbuilding at Levens Hall

A corner of the garden laid out at Levens Hall in the 17th century by the famous garden designer Monsieur Beaumont, who made his home here ▼

▲ The head of Longsleddale. This is one of the least known of the valleys. The parallel valley of the Kent is just as remote

LONGSLEDDALE

MAP REF: 89NY4805

Sadgill, near the head of Longsleddale, must be one of the most isolated settlements in the Lake District. The access to the six-mile length of the dale is far to the east of the district, from the A6 north of Kendal, and as such it is less frequented. The River Sprint runs its length. The dale's beauty is in its woodlands, and its craggy head where the road narrows to a rough track, climbing over Gatescarth pass (1387ft) to the head of Haweswater.

Loweswater, one of the chain that includes Buttermere and Crummock Water ▼

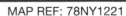

LORTON

MAP REF: 72NY1625

Lorton stands in the fertile vale between Crummock Water and Cockermouth.

The village is divided into two parts. Low Lorton lies in the bottom of the vale on the River Cocker and on the B5289 Buttermere to Cockermouth road. High Lorton stands higher up to the east where the B5292 comes down from the Whinlatter Pass.

Lorton Hall in Low Lorton has a 15th-century pele tower joined to a chapel by a 17th-century frontage and domestic building. It contains priest holes, oak panelling, Jacobean and Carolingian furniture. The public may view the house, which has many historical connections, by appointment (tel. 090 085 252).

The village hall, in High Lorton, is called Yew Tree Hall because of the famous Yew Tree beneath which George Fox, the Founder of Quakerism, preached to a large crowd while Cromwell's soldiers looked on. The great Yew Tree, which stands behind the hall, was immortalised by poet William Wordsworth in his poem *Yew-Trees*.

LOUGHRIGG

MAP REF: 87NY3405

Loughrigg Fell (1099ft) is a prominent feature to the west of Ambleside. Although it covers an area of only four square miles, its complicated structure, with several summits, adds to its attractions to fell walkers. On its north side there are magnificent views over Grasmere, and from Todd Crag, on its southern side, over a long length of Windermere. There is a handsome little tarn below its west side.

LOWESWATER

MAP REF: 78NY1221

The small lake of Loweswater is set delightfully in woodlands. Both lake and woods are in the care of the National Trust. Boats can be hired for fishing. The lake is unique among the others as it is the only one with its waters flowing inland – into Crummock Water. The A5086 to Mockerkin runs along its north shore. The best views of the lake are from the end of Mellbreak south of Loweswater village, and from the village itself there are fine views of the fells.

◄ Although the castle on the Lowther estate is now just a shell and cannot be visited, it is a useful landmark

LOWTHER

MAP REF: 83NY5223

The Lowther estate, on the north-east boundary of the National Park, has had connections with the Lowther family for seven centuries. In the late 17th century Sir John Lowther supported the accession of Protestant William and Mary, and was granted the title of First Earl of Lonsdale.

Lowther Castle was designed by Robert Smirke for the Fifth Earl. The magnificent building was begun in 1806 and finished in 1811. Unfortunately, the upkeep later proved too expensive and the building was pulled down. The magnificent façade remains and is visible, though not approachable, from the roadway on its north side.

The Church of St Michael, across the park to the north of the castle, is 17th-century, but the interior is essentially medieval. In the churchyard is the mausoleum to William, Fourth Earl of Lonsdale (1757-1844), to whom Wordsworth dedicated *The Excursion*.

The Fifth Earl was the great sportsman. The Lonsdale Belt for boxing is still subject to keen competition. He was the 'yellow earl', as he favoured that colour in his livery. He had a yellow Rolls-Royce, and in 1911 he became the first President of the Automobile Association (hence also the Association's yellow livery).

King Arthur's Round Table: why this circular earthwork is so named is a mystery, as is its origin ▼

Lowther Newtown, to the east of the castle, was rebuilt as an estate village in the late 17th century. A second Lowther, to the south-east, was built between 1765 and 1775, attributed to Robert Adam or his younger brother James.

One hundred and fifty acres of parkland has been developed as a Leisure Park. It offers some easy walks in attractive landscape, with an opportunity to see the red deer herd. The playground area, with a circus, boating lake, rides and many other features, is of special appeal to children. Details of opening times can be had from information centres (or tel. 09312 523).

MAYBURGH AND KING ARTHUR'S ROUND TABLE

MAP REF: 77NY5228

There are the remains of two henges of late Neolithic/Early Bronze Age date between the M6 and the A6 at Eaumont Bridge, south of Penrith. Just to the north of the Pooley Bridge road, B5320, is the Mayburgh circle. It consists of a massive circular bank 15ft high, consisting of many thousands of stones. There is an entrance to the east and there is a single standing stone in the centre – all that remains of a circle of stones whose presence was recorded in the 18th century. Across the road and nearer is the curiously named King Arthur's Round Table. It is assumed that this was built later. Unlike its neighbour, the circle here was constructed by digging a ditch and throwing up a bank. The purpose of the circles, and why they are here so close together remains a mystery. They are in the care of English Heritage.

MIREHOUSE

MAP REF: 73NY2328

In impecunious straits Alfred Lord Tennyson sold his Chancellor's Gold Medal for English Verse for £15 so that he could pay for a journey to Mirehouse. Another regular visitor, Thomas Carlyle wrote 'Mirehouse is

beautiful and so are the ways of it'. Edward Fitzgerald was also a happy visitor. All were friends of James Spedding, a man of letters, who owned Mirehouse, a handsome Georgian home by the eastern shores of Bassenthwaite Lake. A wander down to the estate's lake side might remind one of Tennyson's description of the last hours of King Arthur as he was carried off across the lake in a barge rowed by ghostly figures, with three queens with golden crowns. There is little doubt that the poet was inspired to compose this at this place. A stone and a ring of stone seats, the 'Tennyson Theatre', is used regularly by the Tennyson Society.

See under Keswick, page 63, for opening times of house and grounds.

Dodd Wood, part of Thornthwaite Forest (see page 56), is also in the Mirehouse estate and offers some good walking. Use of the estate is much enjoyed by the nearby Calvert Trust, a training and holiday centre for disabled people.

MUNCASTER CASTLE

MAP REF: 90SD1096

Muncaster Castle gardens are famed for the display of rhododendrons and azaleas in early spring, but there is much of year-round interest. From the terrace there is the surprise of a superb view up into the high central fells. The castle itself is a great attraction. Like many of the border region's stately homes, the earliest part of the present house is a defensive tower which dates from 1325. In 1862 the celebrated architect, Anthony Salvin was employed to design the present splendid building, which balances the old tower at one side with a new one at the other. The castle is rich in treasures. It has its legend. Henry VI, fleeing after his defeat at Towton, is said to have arrived exhausted on to the estate and to have been brought to the castle by shepherds. In thanks for nine days' hospitality he presented his host, Sir John Pennington with 'The Luck of Muncaster', a green glass bowl with gold and enamel decoration. See page 63 for opening times.

▲ London-born Beatrix Potter found happiness and inspiration in her farmhouse at Near Sawrey

Many a literary figure enjoyed Mirehouse and its grounds when it was the home of James Spedding ▼

North of the castle on a by-way east of the A595 is the reconstructed 18th-century Muncaster Mill. The 13ft wheel and grindstones turn again, to grind corn into flour which is sold on the premises.

NEAR SAWREY

MAP REF: 93SD3795

This village on the edge of Esthwaite Water has been immortalised by the fame achieved by Beatrix Potter.

The authoress first came to Near Sawrey in 1896 when her parents rented a furnished house in the village called 'Lakeland' (now 'Ees Wyke'). After describing the village 'as nearly perfect a little place as I ever lived in', she bought 'Hill Top', a 17th-century farmhouse, with the help of royalties from *The Tale of Peter Rabbit* (1900) and eventually made it her home.

Several of her subsequent tales were written while she was living at 'Hill Top', including some of the most popular ones such as *Tom Kitten* (1907), *Jemima Puddleduck* (1908) and *Samuel Whiskers* (1908). Six of her stories were specifically connected with the house.

'Hill Top' (National Trust) is now a museum, kept in the style in which she (and her animal friends) knew it. It contains her china, furniture, pictures and original drawings.

Owing to the small size of the house, it may be necessary to restrict numbers visiting at any one time; delays may occur at peak viewing times. There is a small layby opposite 'Hill Top', but a larger parking area past the adjacent 'Tower Bank Arms', the inn which is pictured in *The Tale of Jemima Puddleduck*. (also in the care of the National Trust).

MAP REF: 79NY2420

Every valley, said Wordsworth, has its distinct and separate character. The Newlands valley is very different from the nearby Borrowdale valley. Settlement is so scattered that, apart from a few farms, there are only two small hamlets, Stair and Littletown.

Littletown, aptly named, was immortalised in Beatrix Potter's *Tale of Mrs Tiggy Winkle*, where its buildings feature in some of the drawings. The farm of Stair has the inscription TF1647. It is said that Thomas Fairfax, commander of the Parliamentary forces in the Civil War, stayed there.

Duddon Sands in AD540. It is now a popular little tourist village.

St Patrick's Church, built in 1853, is notable for its tapestries by Ann Macbeth, embroideress extraordinary, who lived in Patterdale from 1921 until her death in 1948 aged 73.

She had a house, High Bield, built high on the rocks above Hartsop, but she left that mainly for her nephews and nieces. She herself stayed or made her home in several houses in the dale, including Wordsworth Cottage. From there came inspiration for her two famous wall hangings, including one with the musical notes of Hubert Parry's *Jerusalem* (the Women's Institute 'hymn') embroidered on it. After this

Summer Bank Holiday Saturday, these brilliantly demonstrate the ability of man and dog to work together to control and manage a group of sheep.

MAP REF: 77NY5130

Penrith is a busy market town north-east of the National Park boundary (pop. 13,200), serving a large farming area. Its strategic importance on the south-north route (A6) was recognised by the Romans who built a fort, *Voreda*, north of the present town. Penrith was too near the disputed border for comfort. It was burned by the Scots in 1314, in 1345

▲ There is little evidence to be seen now of the mining that once took place in sparsely populated Newlands valley

Mining had started in the valley at the time of Queen Elizabeth I. Rich veins of copper and lead, even a little gold, were found on the fells of Catbells and Maiden Moor on the east side of the valley.

The ravages of mining have now been healed by nature, although one can discern grassy spoil heaps and mossy adits. The splendour of this valley makes it a favourite spot with visitors.

One very interesting natural feature on the road over to Buttermere is the Keskadale Oak Wood above Keskadale. This has considerable scientific importance because it may be one of the few surviving relics of primeval forest which once covered Lake District fells.

MAP REF: 82NY3915

Patterdale was named after St Patrick, who is said to have walked here after being shipwrecked on the

was admired by Queen Mary at a London exhibition, it was given to Patterdale Church so that it would stay in the dale which inspired it.

Patterdale is well known for its Sheep Dog Trials. Held on the Late

Shepherds' crooks being judged at Patterdale Sheep Dog Trials ▼

and again in 1382. When Ralph Neville received the town and manor from Richard II the fortification was extended and improved. Later occupants were Richard, Earl of Warwick ('the Kingmaker') and Richard Duke of Gloucester (later Richard III), when he was Warden of the Border's Western Marches. Today

▲ The clock-tower in Market Square at the centre of Penrith

THE BORDER RAIDERS

The border area between England and Scotland was a problem area even in Roman times, and it remained so for another 1500 years. The border line was a matter of long dispute. Battles between England and Scotland were fought at regular intervals through the centuries. After Bannockburn Robert the Bruce's forces devastated the area, burning the towns and sacking Furness Abbey and the priories. When some stability returned the wealthier landowners built defensive 'pele towers', into which families and precious farm breeding stock could retreat in the event of further Scottish raids. Some pele towers have survived, occasionally as part of the more luxurious houses built from the 17th century.

To arrange the defence of the area 'Wardens of the Marches' were appointed by the crown. By law the area's landlords required their tenants, at their own expense, to equip themselves with arms, body armour, and horse; and to respond and report at an hour's notice, 'upon warning given by firing of a becon, post or proclamation by the Lord Warden of the Marches'. The service given by the tenants was to the crown, not the landlord. This gave to many of them and their heirs unusually privileged tenancy rights which served them well in later centuries.

Major Scots incursions were not the only concern. Armed gangs of cattle raiders plagued local farms until the 17th century, when the severe policy of James I brought some stability to the border and the people could at last go about their business in peace.

One of the most impressive examples of a border pele tower built to keep the Scots at bay was Dacre Castle in the Eden valley. It was restored in 1675 ▼

the south wall still stands with parts of the eastern towers.

St Andrew's Church was burned with the rest of the town, but the thickness of the early Norman tower walls ensured its survival. What is now seen is largely the rebuilding of the 18th century. In the churchyard is the 'giant's grave'. A tradition is that it is the grave of Caesarius, King of Cumbria in the 10th century. Actually it consists of Angle or Norse cross shafts at the ends, with 'hogback' gravestones.

There are interesting old buildings in the town. One is the building dated 1563 in which Dame Birkett kept school and where William and Dorothy Wordsworth, aged seven and six, were taught when they lived with their grandparents in Devonshire Street. The Gloucester Arms dates from the 15th century, and is said to have been occupied by Richard of Gloucester. The George Hotel was the lodging of Bonnie Prince Charlie during the '45 rebellion.

There is a Steam Museum in the town, with several steam engines and a collection of agricultural and engineering equipment. There is a small town museum at Robinson School in Middlegate, which also houses the information centre.

PILLAR

MAP REF: 78NY1712

Pillar is a prominent fell, rising to 2927ft, above the head of Ennerdale. It is named from a detached gnarled, folded and buttressed 590ft-high pillar of rock on the fell's northern side. It was first climbed in 1826 and has been a popular challenge to rock climbers ever since. The ascent of the fell, however, offers no problems and the views are exceptional.

Penrith Castle, standing in Castle Park ▶

▲ The Ravenglass and Eskdale
Railway

RAVENGLASS

MAP REF: 90SD0896

Ravenglass is a very attractive west
coast village within the National
Park.

The Romans made it their naval
base for the whole of their
occupation of north-west England.
They built a fort there, just south of
the present village, in AD78, which
accommodated 1000 men. It
remained in use for about 300 years.
The Bath House, known as Walls
Castle, is one of the highest standing
remains of a Roman building in this
country (and it can be seen on a
short walk from the village).

Ravenglass was given a market
charter by King John in 1208, and it
continued to flourish as a port until
the Industrial Revolution, when ports
serving the new major industrial
centres became more important.

In 1875 the Whitehaven Iron Mines
Ltd built a 3ft-gauge railway from the
station at Ravenglass to the Nab Gill
mines at Boot about seven miles up
the valley. A year later it was opened
to passengers. It survived the failure
of the mining company in 1882, but
closed in 1913. Two years later it was
reopened with a 15-inch gauge and a
terminus at Dalegarth just short of
Boot. It continued to carry
passengers and freight, including
granite from Beckfoot quarry, off and
on until 1960. Then when it seemed
the end had come, the railway was
purchased by a Preservation Society.

'La'al Ratty' now provides a daily
service from the end of March to the
end of October (with some trains at
other times), using steam and diesel
engines, to Muncaster Mill, Irton
Road and Eskdale Green, Beckfoot
and Dalegarth/Boot.

On the edge of Ravenglass, just
before the railway bridge, are the car
park and platforms of the Ravenglass
and Eskdale Railway. In the car park
there is a Tourist Information Centre.
Next to the car park is the Ravenglass
Railway Museum, with a slide
presentation as well as historical
details.

Wordsworth landscaped the lovely gardens
at Rydal Mount during his 37 years at the
house ▼

RYDAL

MAP REF: 87NY3606

Rydal was the home of William
Wordsworth from 1813 until his
death in 1850.

Up the hill from the main road in
Rydal is Rydal Mount, to which
Wordsworth brought his family after
they had lived in Grasmere since
1799. He had by then written most of
the poems which made him famous.

The house contains some very fine
family portraits, furniture which
belonged to the poet, personal
possessions and first editions. Next to
the church, where the Wordsworths
worshipped, is the famous 'Dora's
Field'.

On the other side of the hill is Rydal
Hall, which was the home of the le
Flemings, once one of the major
families in the area. It is now owned
by the Church of England as a
Diocesan conference and study
centre, while the grounds are partly
used as a campsite for Boy Scouts
and Girl Guides.

In the grounds of Rydal Hall, on the
Ambleside side, the Rydal Sheepdog
Trials are held on the second
Thursday after the first Monday in
August. The Ambleside Sports are
also held there.

▲ Bluebells beside Rydal Water

▲ Scafell Pike and Wast Water: England's highest peak and deepest lake

St John's in the Vale ▼

John's in the Vale's little church. In the churchyard are some beautifully lettered headstones. One of these commemorates John Richardson (1817-1886) a well-known dialect poet who helped his father build the church school and taught in it for 22 years.

SCA FELL AND SCAFELL PIKE

MAP REF: 85NY2006

Sca Fell (3162ft) is separated from the very much more popular peak of Scafell Pike by the notorious obstacle to walkers, Broad Stand, and a walk between the two is not recommended. Walkers from Wasdale Head bound for Scafell Pike via Brown Tongue and Hollow Stones have a view of the awesome vast expanse and height of the north face of Sca Fell, one of the largest and most important rock climbing crags in Britain. The rock is broken, wrinkled and fissured, and divided by three deep gullies. It was first climbed by the rock climbing pioneers of last century. It claimed lives. Some climbers are buried in Wasdale Head churchyard. There are walkers' routes to the summit, the best, though long, being from Eskdale and up the fell's eastern side by Cam Spout and Foxes Tarn. The view is extensive southwards, but generally inferior to that on Scafell Pike.

At one time all the peaks in this mountain range were known as 'The Pikes of Sca Fell'. What is now known as Scafell Pike (3210ft) is the mountain to the north of Sca Fell (grid ref. NY215072) and is the highest point in England. The summit – a mass of broken slabs and detritus – is often crowded with visitors. Given clarity, the views are tremendous, covering all the central fells. The top was presented to the National Trust by several donors, including the Fell and Rock Climbing Club, as a memorial to the dead of World War I.

The other, slightly lesser pikes – Lingmell, Broad Crag, Ill Crag, and Great End – are comparatively neglected, although the north face of the latter is popular with ice climbers in winter.

The routes to the top of Scafell Pike are long and fairly demanding and should not be attempted if there is a poor weather forecast. Arguably the best and most interesting way from Seathwaite in Borrowdale is via Sty Head Pass (see page 55) and the corridor route on the range's western side. The obvious route from Wasdale Head is via Brown Tongue and Mickledore.

ST JOHN'S IN THE VALE

MAP REF: 80NY3122

A minor road, the B5322, links the A591 north of Thirlmere, with the A66 near Threlkeld, going through a valley by St John's Beck. This is St John's in the Vale. A crag above its southern end is The Castle Rock of Triermain, which (in certain conditions) looks like a ruined castle. Sir Walter Scott travelled this way to visit Wordsworth and the rock inspired the poem *Bridal of Triermain*.

A sign half way along the valley directs one along a narrow way to St

SCOUT SCAR

MAP REF: 95SD4891

The old minor western road from Kendal via Crosthwaite and Cartmel Fell crosses a summit faced with a steep west-facing escarpment. This is Scout Scar and from it there is a surprisingly inspiring panorama of southern Lakeland. The scar is in fact a surviving rim of carboniferous limestone which was chopped short by the moving ice and floods of the Ice Age. The National Park has provided a car park in the summit quarry from which the viewpoint is only a short walk across the road.

▲ Shap Abbey, in a charming setting by the River Lowther west of the town

SHAP

MAP REF: 83NY5615

Shap village is a mile outside the National Park on the A6 between Kendal and Penrith at about 850ft. The area around and the moors to the west were extensively settled in Neolithic/Bronze Age times. There was a stone circle near the village which was destroyed by the railway and other standing stones have been removed, but there is still plenty of evidence of early activity. West of the village, approached by narrow roads and on a secluded site by the River Lowther, are the remains of Shap Abbey (English Heritage). It was founded by Premonstratentions (White Canons) in 1199. After the Dissolution the structure was used as a quarry but the west tower and some walls still stand, and the lay-out of the area can be easily traced.

The famous Shap quarries are south of the village. Now the stone is much used for road works and cement products; but the top quality stone has been used widely in building, including London's St Pancras Station and Albert Memorial.

SIZERGH CASTLE

MAP REF: 95SD4987

Sizergh Castle (National Trust) is west of the A591, 3 miles south of Kendal. The site has been the home of the Strickland family for 700 years of fortune and misfortune. The earliest part of the house is the 14th-century defensive tower. The Great Hall was added in 1450, and there are Elizabethan additions and alterations. Oak panelling dates from this period, but there are five very remarkable

Good Elizabethan carving and fine furniture, plus a superb rock garden, can be seen at Sizergh Castle ▶

still the great crossroads of the fells. It is on the once very busy pack-horse route between Borrowdale and Wasdale, and between Wasdale Head and Langdale. It is now used by fell walkers bound particularly for Great Gable to the west and Scafell Pike to the south.

SWINSIDE STONE CIRCLE
MAP REF: 90SD1788

Swinside Neolithic Stone Cricle, on the lower slopes of Black Combe, is up a lane from the A595 west of Duddon Bridge. It is on private farm land, but can be viewed from the lane, and if necessary approached with permission. If it was less remote it would be well visited, and though it is no keen rival to Keswick Castlerigg for scenery, it is of similar size and is a more complete symmetrical circle of 57 stones.

◀ Tarn Hows is generally acknowledged to be one of Lakeland's prettiest spots. There are a number of classic viewpoints near by

TARN HOWS
MAP REF: 87SD3299

Maps still label the tarn, north of the road between Hawkshead and Coniston, as 'The Tarns', although the tarns became one, long ago, when a dam was built to merge them. The popular name nowadays is Tarn Hows, although that is the name of the nearby farmhouse. Tarn Hows is possibly the most popular beauty spot in Lakeland, visited by almost a million people annually. Its appeal is immediate. A short stride from the car park gives a delightful view over the waters of the tarn, framed in varied woodland, with a background of fells, including the Langdale Pikes. There is an easy walk around the tarn. Tom Heights, to the west of the tarn, is also a classic viewpoint. Tarn Hows was presented to the National Trust in 1930 by the Scott family as a memorial to Sir James and Lady Scott.

carved oak chimneypieces. The house has a fine collection of furniture and paintings.

The gardens are kept exceptionally well and are worth a visit in themselves.

SKIDDAW
MAP REF: 74NY2629

The great bulk of Skiddaw (3054ft) towers impressively over Keswick and Bassenthwaite. Fell walkers who like dramatic-looking crags and rough terrain would regard the ascent as dull, but others who take the smooth with the rough would say its qualities are underestimated. There is no denying the delight of the summit views which can include not only the Lakeland fells, but the Isle of Man, the hills of Scotland and, to the east, the Pennines. One can hardly stray from the popular way up, via the side of Latrigg.

Skiddaw's other peaks offer equally fine prospects: Carl Side, south-west of the summit, gives good views over Derwent Water, and to the west Long Side edge leads to heather-covered Ullock Pike, which some might argue offers the best view of all.

The country referred to locally as 'Back o' Skiddaw' is vast and relatively unfrequented.

STY HEAD PASS
MAP REF: 85NY2109

It used to be said that if a walker should sit by Styhead Tarn long enough he would see all the mountaineers of the world walk past. Nowadays mountaineering covers a rather larger area of the world; but Sty Head Pass, by its lonely tarn, is

TAYLOR GILL FORCE
MAP REF: 79NY2210

There are two routes towards Sty Head from Seathwaite Farm. The less used and rougher one takes the west side of Styhead Gill. This path, in less than a mile, goes upwards by the most wildly spectacular of Lakeland's waterfalls, Taylor Gill Force. The fall is about 100ft in a steep ravine – not a place for anyone with no head for heights.

LAKELAND WEATHER

Wordsworth wrote of what can happen in July and August:

. . . rainy weather, setting in sometimes at this period with a vigour and continuing with a perseverance that may remind the disappointed and dejected traveller of those deluges of rain which fall among the Abyssinian mountains, for the annual supply of the Nile.

It might be true that one can expect to wear waterproofs at the traditional annual holiday times; but the only certainty is the uncertainty. The Lake District has had August droughts and June floods.

The rain gauge on Seathwaite Fell above Borrowdale records the highest rainfall in England: 131 inches average. But the higher fells above could take 150-180 inches. The rain is caused by moist air from the sea in the south-west expanding, cooling and condensing as it is pushed upwards over the fells. Away from the mountains the rainfall falls off rapidly. Rosthwaite, down Borrowdale from Seathwaite, registers only 100 inches; Grange in Borrowdale, in another two miles, 90 inches; while Keswick has 57 inches. The decline continues to the east – Penrith has about 35 inches. The number of wet days in the Lake District, high fells apart, is no greater than in most parts of England. But when it does rain, it rains a bit harder.

The prevailing western winds and the influence of the Gulf Stream mean that the winters are mild. Fell tops apart, the Lake District is not noted for its snowfall. Kent has more snow. Keswick's average temperature compares with London; Grange-over-Sands with the south coast.

THIRLMERE

MAP REF: 80NY3116

Before the 19th century Thirlmere, between Grasmere and Keswick, was sometimes called Leathes Water. It was a narrow lake, bridged in the centre, and there were two hamlets, Armboth in the north, and Wythburn in the south. At the end of the 19th century, in spite of protests, the area was acquired by Manchester Corporation. A dam was built to provide a reservoir and the farms and settlements were flooded. All that now remains of Wythburn is the little chapel which was on higher ground, and which can be seen by the side of the A591. The Corporation planted a forest around the new lake, mainly conifer, a fact which was recently successfully challenged in law as the initial agreement was that native trees would be planted.

Now the offending signs forbidding approach have gone. North West Water has granted access to the lake area and, with cooperation from the National Park Authority, there are lakeside footpaths and picnic areas, reached from the quiet road which Manchester was obliged to construct on the west side. It is even possible to launch light craft (not powered) from a car park at a point which is still called Armboth. The eastern side of the lake has the A591. By Wythburn Church a car park has been made for walkers bound for Helvellyn or wishing to walk northwards avoiding the road side. A further car park for Helvellyn, and forest walks, has been provided three miles to the north, on the right of the road at Swirls. Opposite, on the left of the road, a car park at Station Coppice offers a viewpoint for the lake, and access to a lakeside path.

From the King's Head Inn, at Thirlspot, north-west of the lake, there is another way up Helvellyn which has a long tradition of use.

Manchester's first Lakeland reservoir, Thirlmere ▼

THORNTHWAITE FOREST

MAP REF: 73NY2024

The Forestry Commission was born of the timber shortage after World War I, and one of their earliest plantings, in 1919, was on the south side of Whinlatter Pass, the old road between Keswick and Cockermouth. Since then the forest has been extended up the fells to a height of 1700ft, and northwards on the west side of Bassenthwaite Lake, and to Dodd Wood over the south-east side of the lake. All the plantings were made with scant regard for aesthetics, but now the Commission has responded to criticism by 'softening' the straight boundary lines on the fell sides and by planting more native broadleaved trees. Public access is also encouraged. By the side of Whinlatter (grid ref. NY210246) the Commission have established an imaginative information centre, and there is a choice of recommended walks in the forest.

TILBERTHWAITE GILL

MAP REF: 86NY3000

Tilberthwaite Gill waterfall is approached up a narrow road leaving the A593 Ambleside - Coniston road, 1½ miles north of Coniston. It is in the care of the National Park Authority. A path leaves the small car park by the side of long-abandoned quarries, the gill is crossed and the path reaches a viewpoint bridge for the falls. It is, of course, spectacular after heavy rain. At other times it is just a pleasant walk or a place for a picnic.

TROUTBECK (NEAR WINDERMERE)

MAP REF: 88NY4002

Troutbeck village mainly occupies the western hillside of the Troutbeck Valley two-and-a-half-miles north of Windermere.

In the main settlement there are a number of 17th- and 18th-century farms and houses grouped around wells (piped water was installed only recently).

At the south end of the village is Townend, built in 1626 by George Browne, a yeoman farmer, and occupied by the Browne family until 1944. It is undoubtedly one of the finest examples of a yeoman farmer's house in the Lake District, and it was acquired by the National Trust in 1947.

Townend contains the original home-made carved furniture, domestic utensils and papers of the Browne family, who, along with other landowners, bred and fostered the

◄ *Raven* is one of the two Ullswater steamers that regularly cruise the nine-mile length of the lake. The other is named *Lady of the Lake*

familiar Herdwick sheep which can withstand hard winters and live in upland areas. Their wool was used mainly for rugs, but the National Trust has encouraged the spinning of it into thread suitable for knitting and for weaving into fine wool cloth.

With over 12 houses predating Townend and many other buildings of character in the village, the Lake District Special Planning Board decided in 1981 to make the whole village a Conservation Area. 'Troutbeck is a settlement of outstanding character and value and worthy of conservation,' they said. The area includes the old village school and Troutbeck Church east of the main village by the river and the A592. An interesting feature of the church is the 1873 east window, the combined work of Edward Burne-Jones, William Morris and Ford Maddox Brown, the latter two helping when on holiday in the area.

ULLSWATER

MAP REF: 82NY4220

Ullswater, 7½ miles long, is the second largest lake, and is regarded by many as the most beautiful. Geological changes throughout its length account for its serpentine shape and its varied landscape. The spectacular craggy scenery at the head of the lake, which includes the eastern arms of Helvellyn, the southern end of Fairfield and, close to the east side, the bulk of Place Fell (2154ft) are in the hard volcanic rocks. In the middle reaches are the softer rocks of the Skiddaw slates, and at the foot are the undulating landscapes of limestone and sandstone. A sail down the length of the lake on the service boat (Ullswater Navigation and Transit Co.), preferably north to south from Pooley Bridge pier to Glenridding, reveals all.

Below the northern reach of the lake is the narrow point by Skelly Nab. This takes its name from a rare species of fish, the schelly, which is found only in Ullswater. The fish moves in shoals, and in times past nets were strung across the narrows at this place.

The southern reaches offer the spectacle.

Ullswater is, effectively, a public highway, but there is a 10mph speed limit along its length. Boats are on hire at Glenridding. The A592 runs along the lake's western side, and there are a few small parking areas owned by the National Trust and the Park Authority. A very narrow road runs on the north-eastern side to Howtown, and then makes a tortuous climb into remote Martindale. There is no through road.

From Troutbeck valley the main road heads north up to the Kirkstone Pass. This has been a busy through-route since the Romans started their road over the wild heights of High Street from here and traffic is heavy in season ▼

◄ Ulverston's cobbled market place with its arcaded market house dating from 1736. The church is even older

in 1818 Colonel Thomas Braddyl, succeeding to the estate and finding the place in disrepair, had the present elaborate Gothic house built. In the 1840s the colonel lost his fortune in bad speculation and the house has had a varied history since. Suffering from neglect in the 1970s it was taken over by the Buddhist Manjushri Institute for Tibetan studies who embarked on a scheme of restoration. Visitors are welcome at limited times (see page 64).

ULVERSTON

MAP REF: 70SD2878

Ulverston town (pop. 12,440) was granted its market charter in the 13th century, and on Thursdays and Saturdays its popular market still flourishes. It was long under the control of Furness Abbey.

In the late 18th and early 19th centuries it was a boom town. Iron was mined in the area, notably at Newlands on the town's edge. There were also good supplies of charcoal from lakeland's southern woodlands, and there was water power for the mills. In 1795 there was a scheme to link the town to the sea at nearby Morecambe Bay with a mile-long canal. The engineer John Rennie was responsible for its building and it was opened in 1796. Ulverston then became a busy port, clearing an average of 600 ships a year of 'up to 400 tons burthen'. Maritime industries were encouraged and the population grew to four times its present day level.

The decline was rapid. The development of coke furnaces elsewhere was one reason, but it was the coming of the railway in 1856 which took away the port's trade. There was rapid industrial development too in the new town of Barrow-in-Furness to the south which attracted a population migration. The Furness railway then bought the canal, and it was the end. Now the canal bank offers a pleasant walk for the townspeople.

A prominent landmark above Ulverston is the Hoad monument, in the shape of a lighthouse. It is a monument to local-boy-makes-good Sir John Barrow (1764-1848) author, explorer and Under-Secretary to the Admiralty for 40 years.

The oldest building is Swarthmoor Hall. This became a base for George Fox (1624-1691), founder of the Society of Friends (Quakers), when he was preaching in the region.

Ulverston treated him badly, even violently, but Judge Fell, the owner of Swarthmoor Hall, though not a Fox convert, gave him hospitality. Eleven years after Judge Fell's death George Fox married Margaret Fell, the widow and a committed convert, and Swarthmoor became home, though both George and Margaret suffered persecution for their beliefs and spent periods in prison. The house is owned by the Society of Friends and is open to the public (see page 64).

On the fringe of Ulverston on the coast road is Conishead Priory. At the Dissolution the 12th-century priory was demolished and a house built by the second Lord Monteagle. In the 17th century it had passed into the hands of the Braddyl family, who entertained royalty at the house; but

WASDALE AND WAST WATER

MAP REF: 84NY1606

As one travels from Gosforth in the west, the first view of Wasdale makes an immediate impact. Straight ahead is the great crumbling 1500ft rock wall of the Wast Water Screes, falling into the deepest lake in England. For some this scene is too austere, even vaguely hostile. To the left there is another startling prospect – of high fells shoulder to shoulder around the lake head.

The three-mile-long lake is the deepest in England. Those screes continue their downward incline to a depth of 250ft. The water is pure, so much so that it sustains little freshwater life, though there are char and brown trout.

Although home to a community of Buddhist monks nowadays, Conishead Priory is open to visitors who can enjoy guided tours of the house and walks in the grounds ▼

▲ Great Gable at the head of Wast Water. The National Trust own the lake, including the bed lying 58ft below sea level

The settlement – a little church, a hotel and a few farms – is at Wasdale Head. Much of this area is in the care of the National Trust. The hotel gave hospitality to the pioneer rock climbers and mountaineers exploring the crags, particularly on the Sca Fell and Great Gable areas at the dale head, in the 19th century. It is still the climbers' hotel. The old church is one of England's smallest. Like a small barn, it has a unique atmosphere. There is a tiny window which appropriately has a panel with the words 'I will lift up mine eyes unto the hills'. It used to be claimed that the church's timbers came from a wrecked ship of the Spanish Armada. In the graveyard are a number of memorials to climbers killed in accidents.

Behind the hotel is a fine example of a little stone arch bridge. This is the beginning of a track which goes between Yewbarrow (2058ft) and Kirk Fell (2630ft) by Mosedale to the Black Sail Pass and Ennerdale. Directly on from the Wasdale Head, though, is one of the main fell tracks which goes up between Great Gable and the Scafells to Sty Head Pass for Borrowdale and Langdale. Wasdale Head has the shortest route to Scafell Pike.

The only other settlement is at Nether Wasdale. The church here is worthy of a visit though it is of no great age. It has texts on its ornate ceiling, and 17th-century oak carvings from York Minster.

WATENDLATH

MAP REF: 80NY2716

The narrow road to the hamlet of Watendlath leaves the Borrowdale road on the east side of Derwent Water at Ashness Gate. It crosses the scenic Ashness Bridge, and goes by Surprise View and Ashness woods. In many stretches it is single-vehicle width. The settlement, which consists of a few farms by the attractive Watendlath Tarn, can be reached directly on foot from Rosthwaite in Borrowdale. Readers of Hugh Walpole's *Rogue Herris* novels will associate Watendlath with Judith Paris. Judith's house is by the tarn.

WHINLATTER PASS

MAP REF: 73NY2024

The old road between Keswick and Cockermouth did not skirt Bassenthwaite Lake as at present, but went by the more direct steep route over Whinlatter Pass from Braithwaite. The road (B5292) is now largely used as an easier route from Keswick to Loweswater, Crummock, and Buttermere. The road rises to over 1000ft. At its eastern end there are good views over Bassenthwaite Lake and across to Skiddaw. It passes through Thornthwaite Forest (see page 56) and descends into Lorton Vale on its western side.

Wasdale Head, north of Wast Water, a centre for climbers ▼

WINDERMERE (LAKE)

MAP REF: 93SD3996

Windermere is the largest lake in England – 11 miles long – and one of the most beautiful. The lake sides are largely wooded, particularly on the western side in the middle reaches, and there are wooded islands, which all offer pleasing colours in spring and autumn. It is, of course, the most popular lake, is often busy and, to some, noisy with traffic in the holiday seasons; but it remains unspoiled by too much commercialism.

Windermere was ploughed out in the Ice Age by moving glaciers from the high fells to the north. In the northern basin the ice cut downwards to carve out a basin below sea level. Today, after the ages of silting, it is over 200ft deep. Its main feeders are the Rivers Brathay and Rothay, which converge as they enter at the lake head. Its outlet is into the River Leven at Newby Bridge.

Its length is covered by the steamer service from Lakeside at the southern end, to Waterhead, Ambleside, at its northern. Opposite Lakeside on the east side of the lake foot is Fell Foot Country Park (National Trust) with picnic and boating opportunities. Up lake from Lakeside is the busy YMCA's National Centre, offering training and recreation for young people and sometimes families. Along much of the west shore of the lake, from this point northwards to the ferry, there is a public footpath.

The ferry, which has an ancient history, links Bowness with the road to Hawkshead via the Sawreys and Esthwaite Water. The resort of Bowness is the lake's major centre of activity, with boat hire and launching facilities, a busy promenade and lakeshore access.

Here the lake is almost divided by Belle Isle. The island in old times held the manor house, though evidence has been found of Roman occupation. During the civil war it was in the ownership of the Royalist Philipsons, and was besieged unsuccessfully for 80 days during the absence, on another campaign, of Colonel Huddleston Philipson (nick-named 'Robin the devil'). The colonel disgraced himself by riding his horse into Kendal Church during worship in the search for his Cromwellian foe, Colonel Briggs. In 1774 the island was acquired by a Mr English who caused the present round house to be erected. The incongruous architecture was much criticised and he sold the property to Isabella Curwen, heiress to a West Cumberland mining fortune. She and her husband planted the surrounding trees, and also the large area on the steep slopes of the western side of the lake, Claife Heights, now in the care of the National Trust.

Just north of Bowness is the Steam Boat Museum, which houses some of the historical boats, including some steam-powered, which once plied the lake. In mid-lake are several attractively wooded islands, Thompson Holme, and two named 'Lilies of the Valley' (National Park Authority). Just north again on the eastern side is Miller Ground landing, and the hill above, Adelaide Hill (National Trust), is one of the best viewpoints for the lake. A ferry once plied from Miller Ground to Belle Grange on the western shore.

Three miles up lake from Bowness on the eastern side is the National Park Visitor Centre, Brockhole (see page 27). Wray Castle (page 61) is opposite. Here is the deepest part of the lake and the most scenic. Just north again on the east side, is the Low Wood Hotel, once an old coaching inn, from which point there is a picture-postcard view of the Langdale Pikes across the lake. At Waterhead there are the steamer and boat landings for Ambleside.

Windermere is effectively a public highway and it is the only lake not subject to an overall 10mph speed limit, though there are of course speed limit areas which are marked. The lake is policed and wardened.

The lake is well stocked with fish, including a deep-water trout, the char. Windermere potted char was once a greatly favoured delicacy on the tables of the 17th and 18th-century aristocracy. Char fishing, with a spinner, is a special art.

WINDERMERE (TOWN)

MAP REF: 94SD4198

Windermere town is a mile from the lake at Bowness. It was called Birthwaite until the railway reached it in 1847. The intention was that the line would continue to Ambleside but this was thwarted by the efforts of the conservationists of the day (including William Wordsworth) and influential landowners. Whoever heard of Birthwaite? The railway company

Fell Foot Park. This 18-acre country park on the shores of Windermere offers fishing, boating, bathing, a café, a shop and an information centre ▼

THE EARLY TOURISTS

In the improved economic climate of the 18th century increasingly large numbers of the well-to-do did the 'Grand Tour' of Europe. There was an appreciation of fine landscape which the popular paintings of such artists as Claude Lorraine, Salvator Rosa, and Poussin helped to romanticise and popularise. The unsettled state of Europe in the latter half of the century, and an increased sense of patriotism, led to a search for fine landscape nearer to home, and the Lake District was 'discovered'.

The artists came in numbers. Gainsborough painted and drew here in 1783. JMW Turner made his first tour in 1797, and returned to make a number of paintings. John Constable came in 1806, staying with skilled, though amateur artist John Harden at Brathay, Ambleside. Constable made some 70 watercolours and sketches. He wrote below one

'The finest scenery that ever was', but he made only the single visit, finding the mountains 'oppressive'.

Encouraged by best-selling guide books, such as that written in 1778 by Father West, a local Jesuit priest, and by Wordsworth in 1810, the popularity of the Lake District grew and tourism became a local industry. The tourists of the day did not look at the view 'raw'. They carried small, tinted mirrors in handsome frames, and they stood with their backs to the view, held the mirrors above them, and saw the scene suitably contained. Because what they saw looked something like a Claude Lorraine painting, they called the mirror a 'Claude glass'.

called its station Windermere, and the present town, with hotels and guest houses, grew rapidly as a Victorian resort. All the buildings of this period and since have utilised the attractive local stone and slate. Some of the larger houses, once owned by industrialists, have been converted to hotels. One, on the Troutbeck road out of the town (A592), is now the Lake District Cheshire Home, and its gardens, open to the public, are in the care of the Lakeland Horticultural Society.

There are some good viewpoints. School Knott, east of the town is one; but Orrest Head, above the town to the north and easily reached by a path opposite the railway station, is one of the best viewpoints in the whole of the Lake District. It commands the long lake lengths and most of the central fells and, to the east, includes the fells of the Yorkshire Pennines.

WRAY CASTLE
MAP REF: 87NY3700

Wray Castle, on the western side of the upper reaches of Windermere, from a viewpoint east of the lake, looks impressively medieval. In fact it is a piece of Victorian architectural extravaganza. The grounds even included romantic mock ruins. It was built for a Liverpool surgeon, Dr James Dawson, in the 1840s. It is now in the care of the National Trust, who, for public safety reasons, demolished the ruins. The grounds

running down to the lake shore are a great attraction. The castle is tenanted by a Merchant Navy training school and is not open to the public.

The church, built with the castle, was served for a time by the talented Canon Hardwicke Rawnsley, who later was the incumbent at Crosthwaite Church in Keswick, and became the champion of the Lake District conservationists, and the inspiration and founder member of the National Trust.

West of Wray is the attractive Blelham Tarn, a nature reserve.

View from the grounds of Wray Castle on the edge of Windermere ▼

WRYNOSE PASS
MAP REF: 86NY2702

The narrow road from Little Langdale to the head of Dunnerdale by Cockley Beck, and to Hard Knott Pass and Eskdale, climbs very steeply to 1281 feet, over Wrynose Pass. The Roman Road to Hardknott fort from Ambleside came this way.

On the pass summit is the 'Three Shires Stone', for it is here that three of the old counties met. To the south, are the slopes of the Coniston Old Man range, in Lancashire. To west and north is Cumberland. To the east and north Westmorland. Wrynose is the source of the River Duddon to the west, and the Brathay to the east.

CONTENTS

Places to Visit
Stately homes, castles, gardens, museums, and other attractions

Sports and Activities
Angling, boating and lake cruises, cycling, golf, riding, and trekking, sailing, walking, watersports

Craft Shops
A selection of workshops where individual items are made

Useful Information
Addresses, National Park information centres, tourist information centres, market days, theatres and cinemas

Customs and Events
A calendar of events

◄ Amateur cycling races at Ambleside Sports. This popular occasion, held on 1 August, also includes track events, fell racing and Cumberland and Westmorland wrestling

PLACES TO VISIT

Places to visit in the Lake District are listed here under their nearest town or village, and as a rule correspond to the entries in the gazetteer.

The details given are intended to provide a rough guide only to opening times. Very often a place may be open for only part of the day or may close for lunch. Also, although stated as open all year, many places are closed over Christmas and New Year. Full information should be obtained in advance of a visit from a local tourist information centre (see pages 65-6).

Many places are owned by The National Trust or are in the care of English Heritage and, if this is the case, the entry is accompanied by the abbreviation NT or EH.

Telephone numbers are given in brackets.

BH = bank holiday
Etr = Easter

AMBLESIDE

Stagshaw Gardens. *Woodland garden overlooking Lake Windermere.* Open Apr to Jun, daily; July to Oct by appointment.

BARROW-IN-FURNESS

Furness Abbey (EH). 1½m NE of Barrow. *Impressive ruin in lovely setting.* Open Etr to Sep, daily: Oct to Etr, Tue to Sun.

Furness Museum, Ramsden Sq. *History of the area.* Open all year, Mon to Sat.

BOWNESS-ON-WINDERMERE

The World of Beatrix Potter Exhibition, The Old Laundry. *The famous stories brought to life.* Open all year, daily.

Windermere Steamboat Museum, Rayrigg Rd. *Fine collection of steam boats, motor boats and early sailing boats. Trips.* Open Etr to Oct, daily.

CARK-IN-CARTMEL

Holker Hall and Gardens. *Impressive house and gardens with Craft and Countryside Museum and Lakeland Motor Museum.* Open Etr to Oct, Sun to Fri.

COCKERMOUTH

Cumberland Toy & Model Museum, Banks Court. *British toys from 1900 onwards.* Open Feb to Nov, daily.

◄ The sitting room of Wordsworth House furnished in 18th-century style with the original fireplace

Wordsworth House (NT). *The poet's birthplace.* Open Etr to Oct, Fri to Wed.

CONISTON

Brantwood. *Former home of John Ruskin on lake edge.* Open mid-Mar to mid-Nov, daily; winter, Wed to Sun.

The Ruskin Museum, The Institute. *Memorabilia of the writer, plus Ruskin lace.* Open Etr to Oct, daily.

DACRE

Dalemain. *Fine house with three museums and gardens with rare species.* Open Apr to mid-Oct, Sun to Thu.

GRASMERE

Dove Cottage and Wordsworth Museum, Town End. *Wordsworth's home.* Open mid-Feb to mid-Jan, daily.

KENDAL

Abbot Hall Art Gallery. *Period building with extensive collections. Designer and craft workshop.* Open all year, daily.

Kendal Museum of Natural History and Archaeology, Station Rd. *Flora and fauna of the Lakes, people and wildlife from the world.* Open all year, daily.

Museum of Lakeland Life and Industry, Abbot Hall. *Reconstructed workshops, plus Arthur Ransome room.* Open all year, daily.

Sizergh Castle (NT), 3½m S of Kendal. *Elizabethan carvings, furniture and portraits, plus fine rock garden.* Open Apr to Oct, Sun, Mon, Wed and Thu.

KESWICK

Cars of the Stars Motor Museum, Standish St. *Celebrity TV and film vehicles.* Open Mar to Dec, daily.

Cumberland Pencil Museum and Exhibition Centre. *The history of pencil-making from the 1500s to the present.* Open all year, daily.

Keswick Museum and Art Gallery, Fitz Park, *Literary and artistic displays, plus geological exhibits.* Open Apr to Oct, Mon to Sat.

Lingholm Gardens, western shore of Derwent Water. *Formal and woodland gardens.* Open Apr to Oct, daily.

Mirehouse. 3m N of Keswick. *Family house with adventure playgrounds and Victorian nursery.* House open Apr to Oct, Sun, Wed and BH Mons. Grounds open Apr to Oct, daily.

LEVENS

Levens Hall. *Elizabethan home and famous topiary garden. Working steam collection.* Open Etr to Sep, Sun to Thu.

MUNCASTER

Muncaster Castle and Gardens. *House with superb contents. Also centre for the British Owl Breeding and Release Scheme.* Castle open mid-Mar to Oct, Tue to Sun. Gardens open all year, daily.

Muncaster Mill. 1m NW of Muncaster. *Working watermill producing flour and oatmeal.* Open Apr to Oct, Sun to Fri.

NEAR SAWREY

Hill Top (NT). *Beatrix Potter's home.* Open Apr to Oct, Mon to Wed, Sat and Sun.

NEWBY BRIDGE

Fell Foot Park (NT). *Country park with boating, fishing, adventure playgrounds, etc.* Open all year, daily.

Graythwaite Hall Gardens. 4m N of Newby Bridge. *Seven acres with rhododendrons and azaleas.* Open Apr to Jul, daily.

Stott Park Bobbin Mill (EH). *Victorian mill buildings with original machinery.* Open Etr to Sep, daily; Oct to Etr, Tue to Sun.

PENRITH

Penrith Steam Museum. *Engines, farm machinery, smithy, foundry, etc.* Open Etr, Spring BH to Sep, Mon to Fri and BHs.

▼ Muncaster Mill still produces flour and oatmeal in this beautiful setting

Town Museum, Robinson School, Middlegate. *Small museum, local interest.* Open all year, Mon to Sat.

RAVENGLASS

Ravenglass and Eskdale Railway. *Journey through beautiful scenery.* Regular services in season; reduced service in winter.

RYDAL

Rydal Mount. *Wordsworth's final home with 4-acre garden.* Open Mar to Oct, daily; Nov to Feb, Wed to Mon.

SHAP

Shap Abbey (EH). *Ruins from the 13th century.* Open any reasonable time.

SIZERGH CASTLE

See **Kendal.**

SKELTON

Hutton-in-the-Forest. *A major stately home with fine grounds.* House open Jun to Sep, Thu, Fri, Sun and BHs. Grounds open all year, Sun to Fri.

TROUTBECK

Townend (NT). *Fine example of a wealthy yeoman's house with homemade furniture.* Open Apr to Oct, Tue to Fri, Sun and BH Mons.

ULVERSTON

Conishead Priory, Priory Rd. *Gothic mansion being restored. Woodland trails.* Open Etr to Sep, weekends and BHs only.

Laurel and Hardy Museum, 4c Upper Brook St. *Stan Laurel was born in Ulverston, hence this unique museum.* Open all year, daily.

Swarthmoor Hall. *The home of George Fox, founder of Quakerism. Elizabethan manor house with 17th-century furniture.* Open mid-Mar to mid-Oct, Mon, Tue, Wed and Sat. Other times by appointment.

WINDERMERE

See **Bowness.**

SPORTS AND ACTIVITIES

ANGLING

The rivers, lakes and tarns of the Lake District provide excellent fishing. Licences and permits must be obtained, and the permission of the owner or club who has the fishing rights of the water you wish to fish must be obtained beforehand.
  Full information about all aspects of angling in the Lakes can be

obtained from the Regional Fisheries Officer at North West Water (see **Addresses**).

BOATING AND LAKE CRUISES

See also **Watersports** for sailing, canoeing, windsurfing etc.

Coniston. *Coniston Boating Centre,* Lake Road (05394 41366). *Rowing, sailing and motor boats for hire. Steam Yacht Gondola,* Pier Cottage (05394 41288). *Elegant, stylish cruising on Coniston from end-Mar to early Nov.*

Ullswater. *Ullswater Navigation & Transit Co Ltd,* 13 Maude Street, Kendal (0539 721626). *Cruises on Ullswater Apr to Oct. Ullswater Steamers,* Glenridding (07684 82229). *Regular service Etr to Oct.*

Windermere. *Bowness Bay Boating Co Ltd,* Bowness Bay (09662 3360). *Launches operate daily. Windermere Iron Steam Boat Co Ltd,* Lakeside, Newby Bridge (05395 31188). *Daily sailings Etr to Oct.*

CYCLING

Bicycles can be hired at the following places:

Penrith. *Eden Cyclo-Tours,* Unit 8, Redhills (0768 64884).

Satterthwaite. *Grizedale Mountain Bikes,* Grizedale Forest Centre (0229) 860369.

Ulverston. *BikeTreks Mountain Biking,* Abbots Reading Farm Cottage, Haverthwaite (05395 31835). *Red Lion Inn,* Lowick Bridge (022985 366).

Windermere. *Windermere Cycles,* The Gallery, South Terrace, Bowness (09662 4479).

GOLF

The following clubs and courses welcome visitors:

Bowness-on-Windermere. *Windermere,* Cleabarrow, 1m E of Bowness (09662 3123).

Cockermouth. *Cockermouth,* Embleton, 3m E of Cockermouth (07687 76223).

Grange-over-Sands. *Grange-over-Sands,* Meathop Road (05395 33180). *Grange Fell,* Fell Road, 1m W of Grange-over-Sands (05395 32536).

Kendal. *Kendal,* The Heights (0539 724079).

Keswick. *Keswick,* Threlkeld Hall, 4m E of Keswick (07687 79324).

Penrith. *Penrith,* Salkeld Road, ¾m N of Penrith (0768 62217).

Silecroft. *Silecroft,* 1m SW of Silecroft (0229 774250).

Ulverston. *Ulverston,* Bardsea Park, 2m S of Ulverston (0229 52824).

RIDING AND TREKKING

Coniston. *Crook Barn Stables,* Torover (05394 41088).

Hawkshead. *Claise & Grizedale Riding Centre,* Sawrey Knott Estate (09662 2105).

Kendal. *Holmescales Farm,* Old Hutton (0539 729388).

Newby Bridge. *Bigland Riding Centre,* Bigland Hall (05395 31728).

Ullswater. *Rookin House Farm,* Troutbeck (07684 83561). *Side Farm,* Patterdale (07684 82337).

Windermere. *Wynlass Beck Stables,* (09662 3811).

Boats for hire on Windermere ▶

▲ The path from Grasmere to Rydal Water

SAILING

See **Watersports**.

WALKING

The National Park offers the visitor the following guided walks:

Discovery Walks have a theme, such as mining, Beatrix Potter haunts, etc, and are led by an expert in that particular field. A charge is made for these walks, and they may include a boat trip or a pub lunch.

There are also guided walks led by National Park voluntary wardens, and these are free of charge.

Start points and times for all walks can be obtained from any of the national park centres (see below).

WATERSPORTS

A variety of watersports ranging from canoeing to sub-aqua diving is available on the lakes (see also **Boating and Lake Cruises**).

Coniston. *Coniston Watersports,* Lake Road (05394 41760). Sailing and windsurfing centre.

Glenridding. *Glenridding Sailing School,* The Spit (07684 82541).

Kendal. *Lakeland Canoes,* Hollins Lane, Burneside (0539 727051). Kayaks and Canadian canoes for hire. Transportation arranged.

Windermere. *Windermere Sailing Centre,* Leigh Groves Building, Rayrigg Road (09662 88107). *Low Wood Watersports Centre,* Low Wood (05394 34004/33338). Water-skiing, sub-aqua diving and windsurfing.

CRAFT SHOPS

This is just a selection of the many craft workshops to be found in the Lake District.

Ambleside, *Adrian Sankey Glass,* Rydal Road. Traditional and contemporary crystal. *Kirkstone Galleries,* Skellwith Bridge. Lakeland green slate showroom.

Armathwaite, *Eden Valley Woollen Mill.* Quality fabrics and knitwear.

Broughton, *Cartmel Craft Centre,* Broughton Lodge Farm. Resident woodturner, potter, cane restorer, fabric printer, print maker.

Grasmere, *Chris Reekie and Sons Ltd.* Handwoven textiles.

Great Langdale, *The Langdale Craft Shop,* Chapel Stile. Woodcraft, pottery slate, knitwear etc.

Haverthwaite, *Artcrystal,* Low Wood. Engraving, crystal and cut glass.

Penrith, *The Gem Den,* Whitbarrow Village, Berrier. Gemstone jewellery, rocks and fossils. *Wetheriggs Country Pottery,* Clifton Dykes. Working Victorian pottery.

Ulverston, *Cumbria Crystal,* Lightburn Road. Factory producing lead crystal.

USEFUL INFORMATION

ADDRESSES

Cumbria Tourist Board, Ashleigh, Holly Road, Windermere, Cumbria LA23 2AQ (09662 4444).

English Heritage (EH), Bessie Surtees House, 41-4 Sandhill, Newcastle upon Tyne NE1 3JF (091 261 1585).

The Forestry Commission, North Lakes Forest District, Peil Wyke, Bassenthwaite Lake, Cockermouth, Cumbria CA13 9YG (07687 76616).
South Lakes Forest District, Grizedale, Hawkshead, Ambleside, Cumbria LA22 0QJ (0229 860373).

The Lake District National Park Authority, Brockhole, Windermere, Cumbria LA23 1LJ (09662 6601).

The National Trust, The Hollens, Grasmere, Cumbria LA22 9QZ (05394 35599).

North West Water, PO Box 30, New Town House, Buttermarket Street, Warrington WA1 2QG.

NATIONAL PARK INFORMATION CENTRES

All centres are open from Apr to Oct, daily, and have local interpretative displays.

Bowness-on-Windermere, Bowness Bay, Glebe Road (09662 2895).

Coniston, 16 Yewdale Road (05394 41533).

Grasmere, Red Bank Road (09665 245).

Hawkshead, Main Car Park (09666 525).

Keswick, Lake Road (07687 72803).

Pooley Bridge, Finkle Street (07684 86530).

Seatoller, Seatoller Barn (07687 77294).

Ullswater, Glenridding (07684 82414).

Waterhead, Ambleside (05394 32729).

Windermere, Brockhole National Park Visitor Centre (09662 6601). Open end-Mar to Sep, daily.

TOURIST INFORMATION CENTRES

Those marked with an asterisk are not open during the winter.

Ambleside, Church Street (05394 32582).

Barrow-in-Furness, Town Hall, Duke Street (0229 870156).

Cockermouth, Riverside Car Park, Main Street (0990 822634).

Egremont, 12 Main Street (0946 820693).

Grange-over-Sands*, Victoria Hall, Main Street (05395 34026).

Grasmere*, Redbank Road (09665) 245

Kendal, Town Hall, Highgate (0539 725758).

Keswick, Moot Hall, Market Square (07687 72645).

Cumberland wrestlers in action ▶

Penrith, Middlegate (0768 67466).

Ravenglass*, Ravenglass and Eskdale Railway Station (0229 717278).

Ulverston, Coronation Hall, County Square (0229 57120).

Windermere, Victoria Street (09662 6499).

MARKET DAYS

Ambleside
Wednesday

Broughton-in-Furness
Tuesday

Cockermouth
Monday

Egremont
Friday

Kendal
Wednesday and Saturday

Keswick
Saturday

Penrith
Tuesday and Saturday

Shap
Monday

Ulverston
Thursday and Saturday

THEATRES AND CINEMAS

There are theatres at Carlisle, Keswick and Ulverston, and cinemas at Ambleside, Barrow-in-Furness, Carlisle, Keswick, Millom, Penrith, Ulverston and Windermere.

CUSTOMS AND EVENTS

Although the events shown in this section usually take place in the months under which they appear, the actual dates of many vary from year to year.

Numerous other events such as fêtes, flower festivals and horse shows also regularly crop up in the area. Sheep dog trials are a particular feature of Cumbria.

Full details of exactly what is happening where can be obtained from tourist information centres (see pages 65-6) or local newspapers.

MAY

Cartmel Races, Cartmel Race Course (around the Spring Bank Holiday). *Three-day Spring meeting.*

JULY

Cumbria Steam Gathering, Flookborough. *Steam vehicles of all kinds, plus a fairground and stalls.*

Lakeland Rose Show, Flookborough. *Roses, sweet peas, carnations and floral art in abundance.*

For the Grasmere Rushbearing six girls are chosen as Rush Maidens ▼

Rushbearing Ceremony, Ambleside (first Saturday). *A procession of children carrying 'bearings' makes its way through the streets.*

AUGUST

Ambleside Sports, Ambleside (Thursday before first Monday). *Track events, fell races and traditional wrestling.*

Rushbearing Festival, Grasmere (Saturday nearest 5th). *Children carrying rushes process to church.*

Grasmere Sports, Grasmere (Thursday nearest 20th). *Sporting events, dog trails and wrestling.*

Kendal Folk Festival, Kendal. *Two days of concerts, ceilidhs and sing-alongs.*

SEPTEMBER

Egremont Crab Fair, Egremont (third Saturday). *Traditional fair with the World Gurning Championships, plus track and field events.*

Westmorland County Show, Kendal (2nd Thursday). *Agricultural exhibitions, wrestling, carriage-driving, crafts and farm produce.*

OCTOBER

Wasdale Show, Wasdale. *One of Cumbria's premier sheep shows, plus traditional lakeland sports.*

NOVEMBER

Biggest Liar in the World Competition, Santon Bridge. *Held in the Santon Bridge Inn during the evening.*

Kendal Jazz Festival, Kendal. *An assembly of top names perform over a period of two weeks.*

Atlas

▲ Grasmere

The following pages contain a legend, key
map and atlas of the Lake District, three
motor tours and sixteen Lake District walks.

MAP SYMBOLS

THE GRID SYSTEM

The map references used in this book are based on the Ordnance Survey National Grid, correct to within 1000 metres. They comprise two letters and four figures, and are preceded by the atlas page number.

Thus the reference for Coniston appears 92 SD 3097

92 is the atlas page number

SD identifies the major (100km) grid square concerned (see diag)

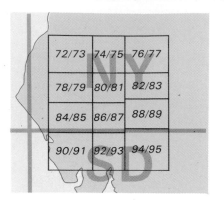

72/73	74/75	76/77
78/79	80/81	82/83
84/85	86/87	88/89
90/91	92/93	94/95

3097 locates the lower left-hand corner of the kilometre grid square in which Coniston appears.

30 can be found along the bottom edge of the page, reading W to E

97 can be found along the right hand side of the page, reading S to N

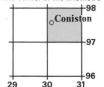

ATLAS 1:63,360 – 1" TO 1 MILE ROADS, RAILWAYS AND PATHS

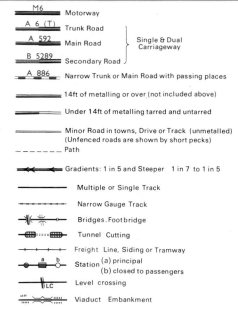

M6 — Motorway

A 6 (T) — Trunk Road

A 592 — Main Road ⎫
B 5289 — Secondary Road ⎬ Single & Dual Carriageway

A 886 — Narrow Trunk or Main Road with passing places

— 14ft of metalling or over (not included above)

— Under 14ft of metalling tarred and untarred

— Minor Road in towns, Drive or Track (unmetalled) (Unfenced roads are shown by short pecks)

— — — — Path

Gradients: 1 in 5 and Steeper   1 in 7 to 1 in 5

— Multiple or Single Track

Narrow Gauge Track

Bridges. Footbridge

Tunnel Cutting

Freight Line, Siding or Tramway

Station (a) principal
(b) closed to passengers

Level crossing

Viaduct Embankment

PUBLIC RIGHTS OF WAY

—·—·—·—·— Road used as a Public Path

·+·+·+·+·+·+ By-way open to all traffic

················ Footpath

— — — — — Bridleway

Public rights of way indicated by these symbols have been derived from Definitive Maps as amended by later enactments or instruments held by Ordnance Survey on 1st October 1990 and are shown subject to the limitations imposed by the scale of mapping.

Later information may be obtained from the appropriate County Council.

The representation in this atlas of any other road track or path is no evidence of the existence of a right of way

Danger Area   MOD Ranges in the area. Danger! Observe warning notices

BOUNDARIES

+ — + — National   ·—·—·— County

National Park   + + + District

NT National Trust   NT always open
NT opening restricted

FC Forestry Commission   Pedestrians only - observe local signs

GENERAL FEATURES

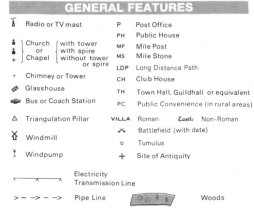

Radio or TV mast   P   Post Office
                          PH   Public House
Church ⎰ with tower   MP   Mile Post
or ⎱ with spire   MS   Mile Stone
Chapel   without tower   LDP   Long Distance Path
         or spire   CH   Club House
○ Chimney or Tower   TH   Town Hall, Guildhall or equivalent
Glasshouse   PC   Public Convenience (in rural areas)
Bus or Coach Station
△ Triangulation Pillar   VILLA Roman   Castle Non-Roman
                          ⚔ Battlefield (with date)
Windmill   ☆ Tumulus
Windpump   + Site of Antiquity

Electricity Transmission Line

> — > — > Pipe Line   Woods

Quarry   Orchard

Spoil Heap or Refuse Tip   Park or Ornamental Grounds

WATER FEATURES

Marsh or salting
Towpath Lock
Aqueduct Canal   Ford
Lake Weir Footbridge Bridge Normal tidal limit
═════════ Canal (dry)

HEIGHTS AND ROCK FEATURES

outcrop   cliff 500
                 250   scree

Contours are at 50 feet vertical interval

To convert feet to metres multiply by 0·3048

Heights shown close to a triangulation pillar refer to the station height at ground level and not necessarily to the summit

TOURS

2   Start point of tour   Featured tour

➤ Direction of tour   6 Point of Interest

TOURIST INFORMATION

Camp Site   Nature reserve
Caravan Site   Other tourist feature
Information Centre   Preserved railway
Parking Facilities   Racecourse
Viewpoint   Wildlife park
Picnic site   Museum
Golf course or links   Nature or forest trail
Castle   Ancient monument or Historic building
Cave   Places of interest
Country park   Telephones
Garden   PC Public Convenience
Historic house   Youth Hostel

Mountain Rescue Post with telephone and supervisor

Mountain Rescue Kit Equipment only

TOURS 1:250,000 – ¼" TO 1 MILE ROADS AND RAILWAYS

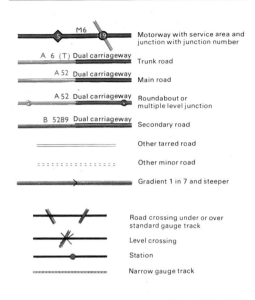

M6	Motorway with service area and junction with junction number
A 6 (T) Dual carriageway	Trunk road
A 52 Dual carriageway	Main road
A 52 Dual carriageway	Roundabout or multiple level junction
B 5289 Dual carriageway	Secondary road
	Other tarred road
	Other minor road
	Gradient 1 in 7 and steeper

Road crossing under or over standard gauge track

Level crossing

Station

Narrow gauge track

WATER FEATURES

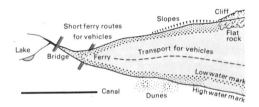

Cliff
Slopes
Short ferry routes for vehicles
Flat rock
Lake
Bridge
Ferry
Transport for vehicles
Low water mark
Canal
Dunes
High water mark

GENERAL FEATURES

Buildings

⊕ Civil aerodrome (with custom facilities)

Wood

Ⅰ Radio or TV mast

Lighthouse

ʕ ʕ Telephones : public or motoring organisations

ANTIQUITIES

Native fortress

------ Roman road (course of)

Castle • Other antiquities

CANOVIVM • Roman antiquity

RELIEF

Feet	Metres	
		.274 Heights in feet above mean sea level
3000	914	
2000	610	
1400	427	Contours at 200 ft intervals
1000	305	
600	183	
200	61	
0	0	To convert feet to metres multiply by 0.3048

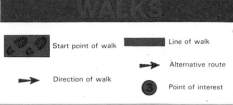

WALKS

Start point of walk

Line of walk

Direction of walk

Alternative route

③ Point of interest

WALKS 1:25,000 – 2½" TO 1 MILE ROADS, RAILWAYS AND PATHS

M I	M I	Motorway	.... Path
A 64(T)	A 6(T)	Trunk road	Narrow roads with passing places are annotated
A 515	A 57	Main road	
B 6465	B 6105	Secondary road	
A 6(T)	A 57	Dual carriageway	
		Road generally more than 4m wide	
		Road generally less than 4m wide	

Multiple track		Level crossing
Single track		Cutting
Narrow Gauge		Embankment
Road over & under		Tunnel
Siding		

Permitted path and bridleway — — — — Paths and bridleways along which landowners have permitted public use but which are not public rights of way The agreement may be withdrawn.

Access Land | Access Land | Land open to the public by permission of the owner
Access Point

GENERAL FEATURES

Church or Chapel	with tower / with spire / without tower or spire	° W, Spr Well, Spring
Electricity transmission line pylon pole		Bus/coach station
Gravel pit		Site of antiquity
Sand pit		NT National Trust always open
Chalk pit, clay pit or quarry		NT National Trust opening restricted
Refuse or slag heap		FC Forestry Commission pedestrians only (observe local signs)

HEIGHTS AND ROCK FEATURES

Contours are at 10 metres vertical interval

50 } Determined { ground survey
285 • } by { air survey

Surface heights are to the nearest metre above mean sea level Heights shown close to a triangulation pillar refer to the station height at ground level and not necessarily to the summit

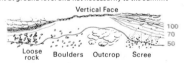

Vertical Face
100
70
50
Loose rock   Boulders   Outcrop   Scree

PUBLIC RIGHTS OF WAY

Public rights of way shown on this Atlas may not be evident on the ground

---------- } Public Paths { Footpath
— — — — } { Bridleway

+++++++ By-way open to all traffic

-+-+-+- Road used as a public path

Where rights of way are co-incident with walks they have been omitted

Public rights of way indicated have been derived from Definitive Maps as amended by later enactments or instruments held by Ordnance Survey between 1st November 1981 and 1st January 1989 and are shown subject to the limitations imposed by the scale of mapping.

The representation on this map of any other road, track or path is no evidence of the existence of a right of way.

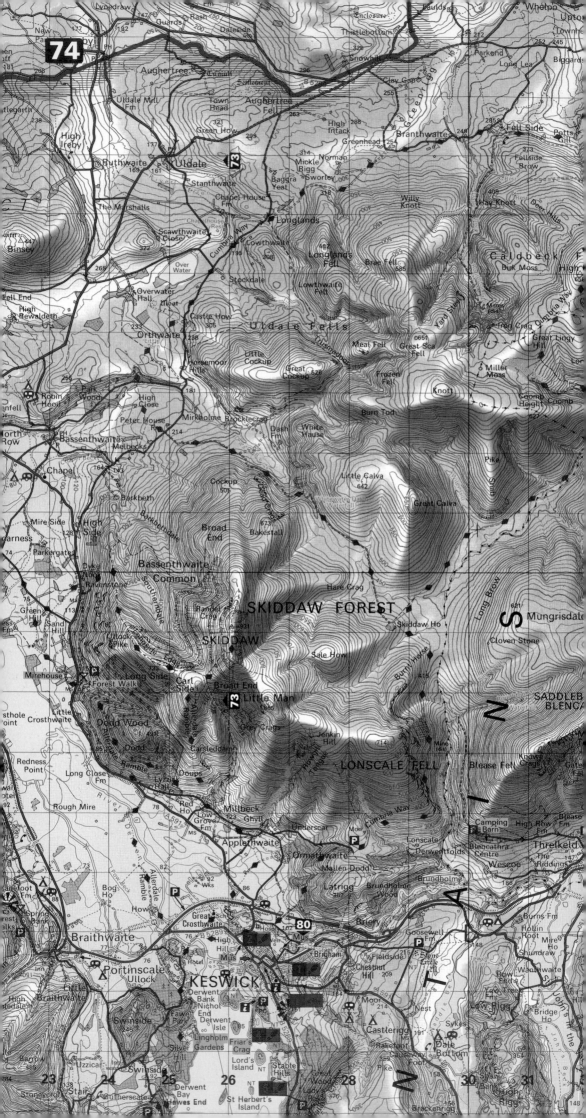

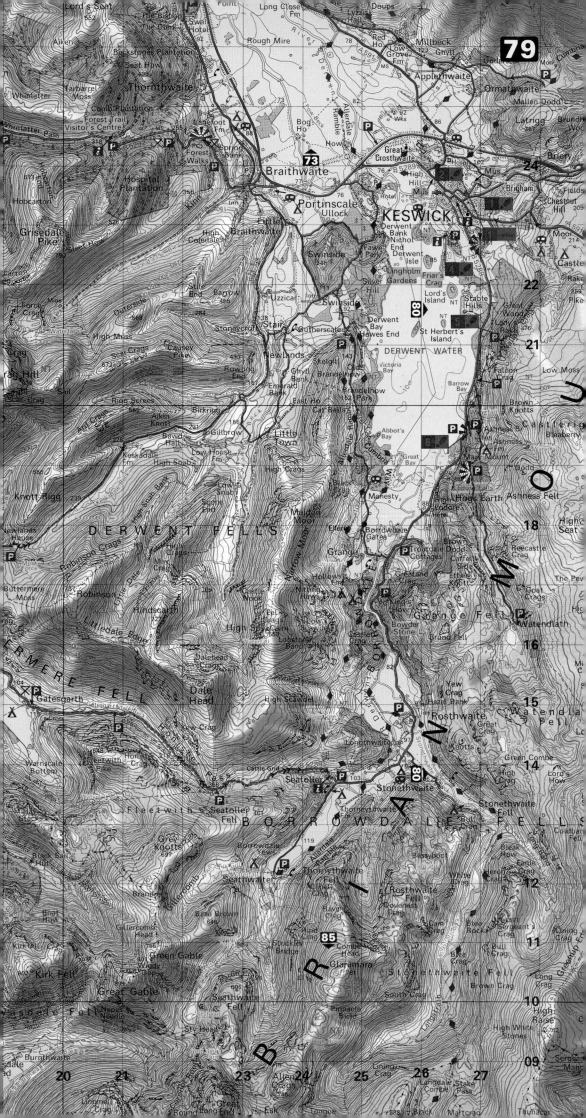

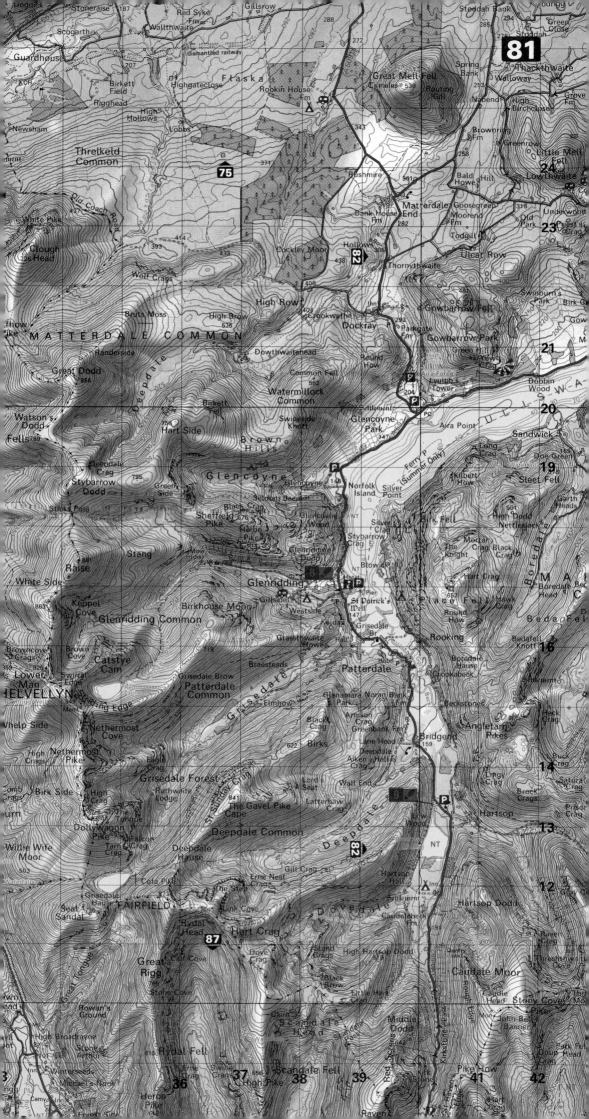

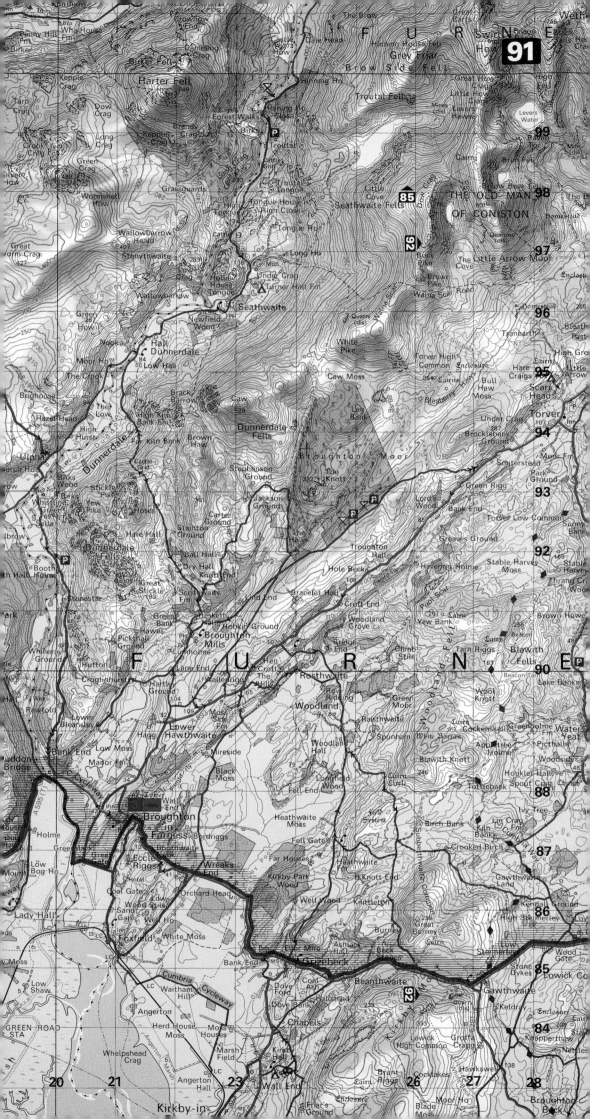

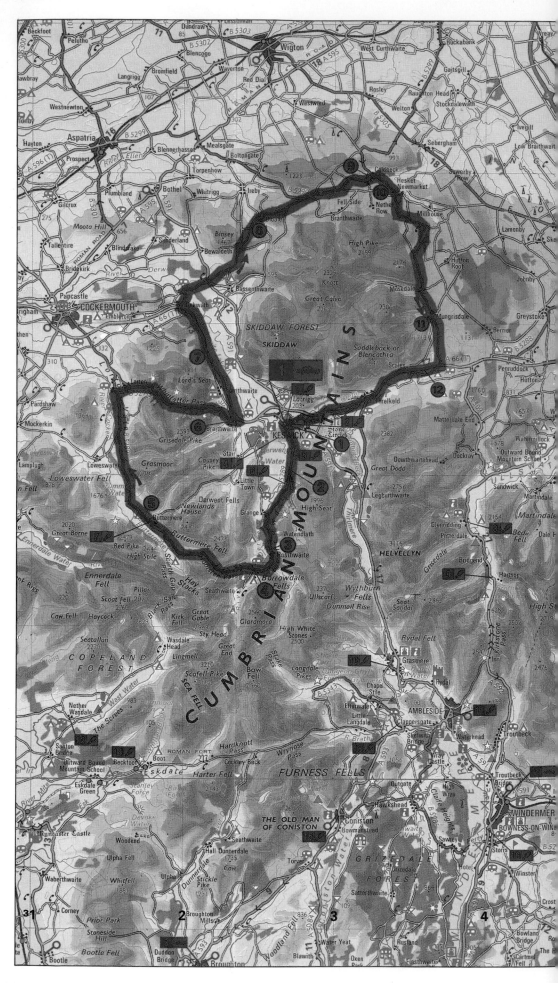

TOUR 1

NORTHERN LAKELAND

From Keswick the tour first visits Derwent Water and wooded Borrowdale, then ascends Honister Pass to dramatic mountain scenery before dropping down to beautiful Buttermere. Another high pass is taken to Bassenthwaite Lake, and then the tour follows quiet open moorland roads in 'John Peel' country.

ROUTE DIRECTIONS

The drive starts from Keswick. 60 miles .

The tour leaves Keswick by the Borrowdale road (B5289) ① .

The road goes along the eastern shore of Derwent Water ② .

Leaving the lake, the road enters Borrowdale ③ .

Continue through Rosthwaite and Seatoller and ascend Honister Pass ④ .

The road goes by Buttermere ⑤ .

After Buttermere the road skirts Crummock Water. Almost 2 miles beyond the lake turn right (signed Lorton, Cockermouth), then in another 2 miles turn right on to an unclassified road and shortly go over the crossroads for High Lorton. At the end of the village turn right, signed Keswick, then at the T-junction turn right again on to the B5292. An ascent is then made over Whinlatter Pass. Descend through Braithwaite village ⑥ .

Turn left (signed Cockermouth A66), then left again on joining the A66. The road goes alongside Bassenthwaite Lake ⑦ .

After 3½ miles, at the far end of the lake, turn right on to the B5291 (signed Castle Inn), then turn right again. In ¾ mile turn right and cross the river bridge. At the Castle Inn turn right, then left over the main road to join the unclassified Uldale road. In 2¼ miles bear right and continue to Uldale ⑧ .

At Uldale go over the crossroads on the Caldbeck road and ascend, then in 2¼ miles join the B5299. After another 1½ miles bear left and continue to Caldbeck ⑨ .

From Caldbeck take the unclassified road for Hesket Newmarket ⑩ .

At Hesket Newmarket bear left, then ½ mile farther bear right, signed Mungrisdale. In 2½ miles pass the Horse and Farrier inn, then cross the river bridge and turn right ⑪ .

At the junction with the A66 turn right, signed Keswick ⑫ .

Follow the A66 and take its branch with the A591 into Keswick.

POINTS OF INTEREST

① Once a mining centre and market town, Keswick is closely associated with the poets Samuel Taylor Coleridge and Robert Southey. Some of their manuscripts, and a good mineral collection, may be seen in the Museum and Art Gallery. See page 63.

② There are steep wooded slopes on the left and excellent views over the lake. Falcon crag, one of the sites popular with rock climbers, is above left.

③ The wooded valley of Borrowdale is at its best in spring and autumn. The conical tree-covered summit of Castle Crag is on the right. There are remains here of a Romano-British fort. As the valley widens, there are views of the crowded peaks ahead. The river is the River Derwent, and it not infrequently floods when there are heavy rainfalls at its source in the highest land in England. This includes Seathwaite Fell, where the average annual recorded rainfall is 131 inches, though above, on the Scafells (out of view), it could be as high as 180 inches a year.

④ Some of Rosthwaite's old farms and buildings are owned by the National Trust. At Seatoller the Lake District National Park has its Dalehead Base, where there are displays and study facilities relating to the geology and geography of the area. The pass rises to 1176ft through mountainous scenery. On the descent there is a spectacular view of Buttermere.

⑤ Buttermere's serene surface is in dramatic contrast with the fells of High Stile, High Crag, and Red Pike towering behind. It is a centre for exploring some of the Lake District's wildest scenery.

⑥ Whinlatter Pass summit is 1043 feet above sea level as it passes through Thornthwaite Forest. On the descent there are views to the left over Bassenthwaite Lake. Braithwaite lies at the foot of the pass.

⑦ There is a good view of Skiddaw (3054 ft) across the lake.

⑧ This gentler undulating country is known locally as 'Back o' Skiddaw' and is famous as the huntsman John Peel's hunting country. Most of Uldale's buildings are 18th- and 19th-century.

⑨ Caldbeck has hardly changed in three centuries. The grave of John Peel (1776-1854) is in the churchyard of the attractive church. The popular song 'Do ye ken John Peel?' was written by John's Caldbeck friend, John Woodcock Graves (there is a plaque on the house where he composed it), and the tune was composed by William Metcalf, the organist at Carlisle Cathedral.

⑩ Hesket Newmarket was known as Hesket until the 18th century when it was granted its market charter and became Hesket Market.

⑪ The road lies under the eastern flank of the Skiddaw massif, passing below the rock face of Carrock Fell (2174 ft) which is crowned with the broken walls of another, large, ancient fort. Mungrisdale Church is dedicated to St Kentigern, otherwise known as St Mungo, after whom the village is named. The church has a very fine three-decker pulpit dating from 1679.

⑫ Blencathra (or Saddleback) (2847ft) is prominent to the right, and at the edge of Threlkeld the road is directly below it.

TOUR 2
THE CENTRAL LAKES AND HELVELLYN

From Windermere the tour goes by Rydal Water and Grasmere, through St John's in the Vale, to Penrith, then along the entire north and western shore of Ullswater, the Lake District's second largest lake.

ROUTE DIRECTIONS

The drive starts from Windermere. 68 miles .

Starting from Windermere (see page 60), go north on the A591 to Ambleside. The road passes Brockhole ① .

Go through Ambleside and continue on the A591 for Grasmere and Keswick, passing Rydal village ② .

Rydal Water is soon in view. Go through White Moss Common ③ .

The road bends and passes Grasmere lake ④ .

Go straight on at the Grasmere crossroads ⑤ .

The road rises to the pass of Dunmail Raise. As it descends on the Thirlmere side, there is very soon an unsigned minor road left. Take this lakeside road ⑥ .

Continue along this minor road ⑦ .

At road junction do not go straight ahead signposted A591 Keswick, but turn right, and drive over the dam. At the A591, turn right signposted Windermere, then soon afterwards take the first turning left, signed Threlkeld B5322 ⑧ .

At the junction with A66 turn right, signed Penrith and Motorway. Continue on and at roundabout go straight ahead signed Brough A66, Penrith (A592), M6. At the next roundabout take the second turning off, signed Penrith A592. At Penrith continue with signs for town centre ⑨ .

From the town centre take the A6 south

signed Shap. At the roundabout take the second turning off, signed Brough A66. Within one mile watch for a minor road on the right, signed Brougham, with an English Heritage sign for Brougham Castle. Take this ⑩ .

Follow the minor road on from the castle. At a cross-roads turn right for Brougham Hall and at the next junction continue right past the hall. Follow the road to its junction with the A6. Turn right, signed Penrith, Ullswater B5320 and then take the first turning left, B5230, signed Ullswater, and Tirril, Pooley Bridge ⑪ .

Go on through Yanwath and Tirril. The road enters Pooley Bridge at the foot of Ullswater. Cross the bridge and continue past the steamer landing stage. At the fork keep left on the A592, signed Windermere. The road continues close to the lake shore, past some viewpoint lay-bys ⑫ .

The Aira Force (NT) is reached ⑬ .

At the junction with A5091, continue on A592. There are excellent views of the hills ahead. Helvellyn is on the right. The road reaches Glenridding ⑭ .

Continuing on past the head of the lake, the road reaches Patterdale. With views of fells ahead, it passes Brothers Water, and then ascends Kirkstone Pass ⑮ .

Continue on A592, past the turning for Ambleside ('the struggle') ⑯ .

Pass Troutbeck Church and reach the junction with the A591 at a mini-roundabout. Go left signed Kendal and Windermere is soon reached.

POINTS OF INTEREST

① Brockhole is the National Park Visitor Centre. It has gardens running down to the lake shore, and displays which help visitors make the most of the Lake District National Park.

② Up the roadway to the right is Rydal Mount, where the poet William Wordsworth lived from 1813 until his death in 1850.

③ This is a popular starting point for many walks in the area.

④ Wordsworth reckoned that the building of this lakeside road damaged the beauty of the area. The old road is above, to the right.

⑤ Dove Cottage, home of the Wordsworths from 1799 to 1808 (open to the public), is just up the minor road on the right.

⑥ This end of the lake is Wythburn, though the village has been under the water since Thirlmere's level was raised to make a reservoir for Manchester in 1894.

⑦ There are a number of small car parks and paths to the lake shore. Across the lake can be seen the great hulk of Helvellyn (3118ft/950m).

⑧ This valley is St John's in the Vale and the fell side on the right is the northern arm of the Helvellyn massif. The impressive mountain straight ahead is Blencathra (or Saddleback).

⑨ Penrith has many historical associations, from the Border wars to the '45 rebellion (see page 50).

⑩ The 12th-century castle (EH) is a spectacular ruin (see page 27).

⑪ There are two henge circles by this junction, one on the left called 'King Arthur's Round Table', one just afterwards on the right, Mayburgh Henge.

⑫ Ullswater is considered by many to be the most beautiful of the lakes, scoring over Windermere with the major mountains at its head.

⑬ Here there is a waterfall in a spectacular gorge (car park and café).

⑭ This is one of the most popular starting points for the ascent of Helvellyn, and is the base for the lake steamers which have a regular service around Ullswater. There is a National Park Information Centre in the car park.

⑮ Kirkstone, at 1500 ft (457m), is the highest road pass in the Lake District.

⑯ There is a glimpse of Windermere to the right, but as the road descends there are spectacular views over the Troutbeck valley to the left.

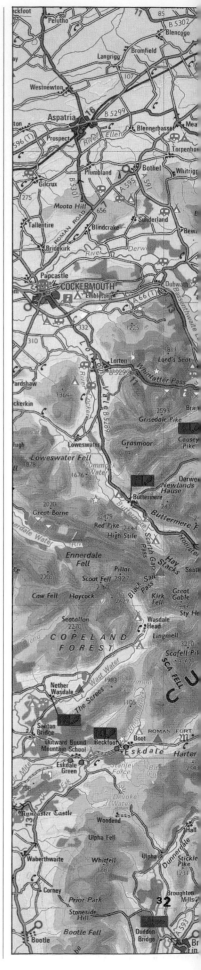

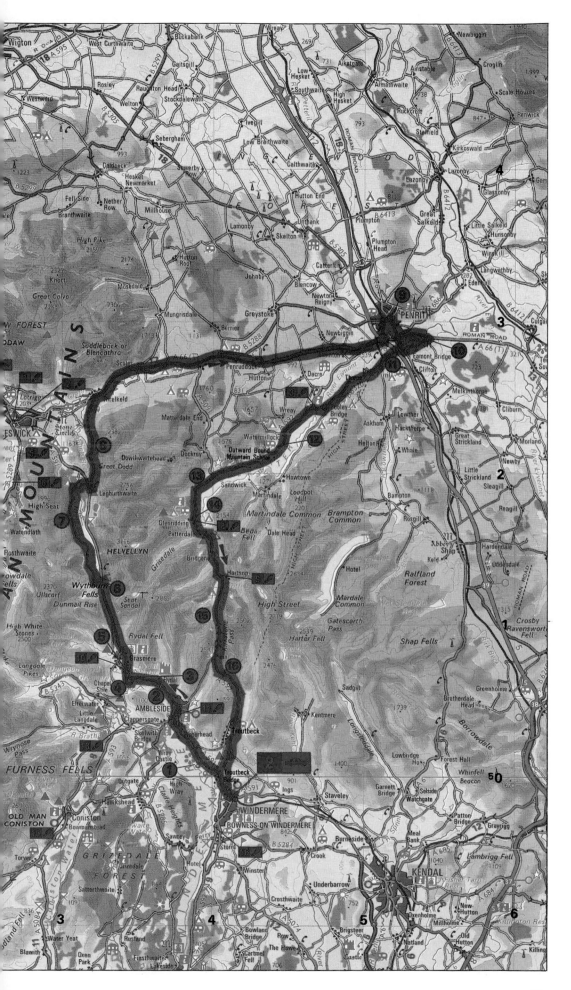

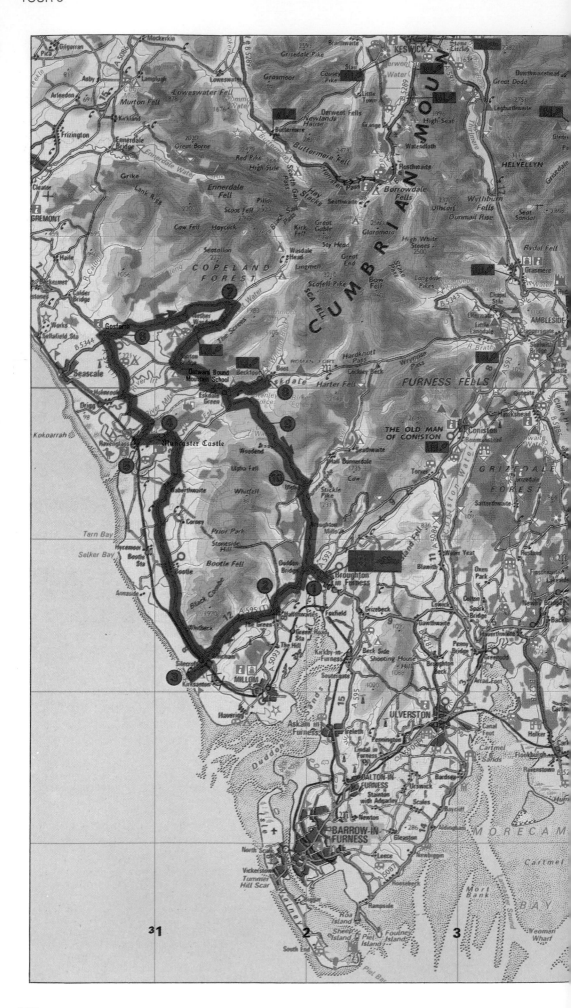

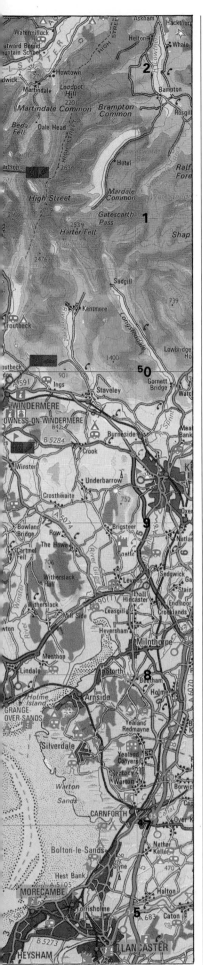

TOUR 3

FROM COAST TO LAKE AND FELL

This tour visits a sandy beach on the rim of the National Park, goes by Muncaster Castle, looks in at the Ravenglass and Eskdale narrow-gauge railway, visits England's deepest lake with the much photographed views of its highest mountains, and finishes via the Duddon, one of Wordsworth's favourite valleys.

ROUTE DIRECTIONS

The drive starts at Broughton in Furness ① . 68 miles .

Leave westwards with the Workington road (A595), across Duddon Bridge and left with Workington sign. At the Millom turning keep on as for Workington ② .
  At the T-junction go left, signed Millom A5093, and shortly afterwards turn right, signed Silecroft. Go over the level crossing and continue to Silecroft beach car park ③ .
  Return to the T-junction and go left for Workington (A595). Go through Bootle and beside Muncaster Castle ④ .
  At the foot of the hill turn left, signed Ravenglass ⑤ .
  Go back to the T-junction and take the Workington road (A595) through Holmrook. At a crossroads turn right, signed Gosforth and Wasdale, and go through Gosforth village. At the next junction go left, signed Nether Wasdale, Wasdale Head ⑥ .
  Go straight on at the road junctions and a T-junction by Wast Water ⑦ .

Continue to the right, on the lakeside road. At the junction turn left for Santon Bridge and left again at a second junction, then left again at T-junction, signed Eskdale, and Broughton. The road rises and passes through forest and then goes through Eskdale Green and past the Outward Bound School. At the junction turn left, signed Boot, Langdale via Hardknott Pass. Drive on to Dalegarth Station at Boot ⑧ .
  Return to Eskdale Green. At the T-junction go left, signed Ulpha and Broughton. The road winds and climbs Birker Fell ⑨ .
  The road reaches Ulpha in Dunnerdale at the foot of a steep hill ⑩ .
  The road follows the river course. At the T-junction turn left, signed Broughton, go past Ulpha Church, then left over Ulpha bridge. The road follows the River Duddon to a T-junction at Duddon Bridge. Go left for Broughton, at the next junction bear left, and then go straight on into Broughton.

POINTS OF INTEREST

① Broughton is an unspoilt village, once an important market town. Broughton Tower, the splendid remains of a castle belonging to the Broughton family, dates originally from the 14th century and was rebuilt in about 1750. The church has Saxon walls and a Norman archway.
② The great bulk of mountain on the right is Black Combe, once described by the Millom poet Norman Nicholson as a 'bowler hat as large as the city of London', and claimed by Wordsworth to have 'a more extensive view than any other eminence the Island affords'.
③ If the weather is clear, the Isle of Man is visible. The sandy beach is impressive and the pebble bank is of great interest to geologists.
④ The castle is open to the public. It dates from medieval times, but was extended in 1862. It is famous for its springtime gardens and views from the terrace walk (see pages 49 and 63).
⑤ Ravenglass is now just a quiet seaside village at the confluence of the Rivers Esk, Mite and Irt, but it was an important port as early as Roman times. Now it is the base for the popular narrow-gauge Ravenglass and Eskdale railway ('Laa'l Ratty'), which has a regular service up Eskdale (see page 52).
⑥ Gosforth churchyard contains a unique, slender 1000-years-old Viking cross with carvings illustrating the Christian story and Norse mythology.
⑦ There is a stunning view of Wast Water Screes, which plunge down 1700 feet from Illgill Head, the fell opposite. They then go down to the lake bed, 250 feet in depth. This is the deepest lake in England. At the head of the lake can be seen something of England's highest land. Great Gable, 2949ft high, looks the most impressive; while the Scafells, which boast the highest point at Scafell Pike (3210ft), is to the right.
⑧ The valley is Eskdale, and this is the terminus for the narrow-gauge railway which originally linked the iron mines and granite quarries hereabout to the port and, later, railway at Ravenglass. It now carries passengers. There is a working corn mill museum in the tiny village. The small church of St Catherine's, set picturesquely by the River Esk, is typical of the old barn-like dales chapels. Stanley Force, an impressive waterfall, is in a wooded gorge to the south.
⑨ There are splendid views from the heights of the pass into the high fells to the north-east. Prominent in the centre distance is the peak of Bowfell, 2960ft above the Langdale valley. Over the moor here are scores of Bronze Age burials.
⑩ 'Ulpha' suggests Norse origins. It might have meant 'Ulf's hay' (park), but a popular theory is that it comes from Norse 'ulf-hauga' or 'wolf hill'. The story of a lady from Ulpha Hall, drowned in the river after being chased by a wolf, might have ancient origins.

WALK 1

LATRIGG AND RAILWAY LINE

The hill which stands dramatically behind Keswick with seemingly impregnable steepness is Latrigg, one of the finest viewpoints in the whole of the Lake District. Its ascent is possible from behind by the easy route described, which finishes along the abandoned railway line through the delightful Greta Gorge.

ROUTE DIRECTIONS

Approx 6½ miles. Allow 2 to 3 hours.
Park in Keswick town centre (grid ref. NY268235).

Leave Keswick town centre via Station Road past the museum, then before reaching the Keswick Hotel turn right along Brundholme Road. Go under the old railway bridge and continue left. At the road junction with a mini-roundabout bear right and continue forward by Briar Rigg. As the way falls take the bridleway right, signed Public Bridleway Skiddaw, and Spooney Green Lane. Cross a bridge over the A66 and continue straight on on an unsurfaced track, ignoring lesser turnings to the right ①.

Eventually the track levels somewhat alongside a conifer plantation, and an obviously well-made terraced path leads off sharply to the right. Take this. The path zig-zags, making ascent to the summit ridge relatively painless ②.

Having enjoyed the view, continue on along a footpath on a low ridge, an old dyke. This reaches a stile. After going over it, continue on a permissive path. It is obscure. To minimise disturbance to sheep, and damage to valuable grassland, go left alongside the fence. On reaching a joining fence, turn right and continue alongside it. This soon meets a more distinct path. Follow this on along another old dyke. This finishes at a fence. Go left with it to join a parallel track by a plantation, at a gate. Go through the gate and follow this track on and down. At the end, at a T-junction, go left, and then descend immediately right, from the gate ③.

Follow this rough roadway down. At the river bridge go right over the little footbridge and on to the abandoned railway line. Go right. Come to one of the old bridges, and a railway hut containing information panels ④.

The track reaches an old railway platform ⑤.

Leave the track by a rising footpath at a point where a tunnel has been filled in. The path turns and goes below the road bridge and eventually rejoins the railway track. Follow this through to the old station. Walk along the platform to the end and turn left, and left again into Station Road.

POINTS OF INTEREST

① As the track rises there are good views of Derwent Water and Bassenthwaite Lake.
② The views all around can only be described as stupendous. Derwent Water and Borrowdale, and, given clarity, most of the central fells, including Scafell Pike, Great Gable and Helvellyn can be seen.
③ The river below left has the strange Celtic name of Glenderaterra Beck.
④ This line, which follows the River Greta, was closed in 1972. It ran from Penrith to Cockermouth from 1864. It was reckoned that the navvies who built it could each move 20 tons of rock and soil a day, on a diet of two pounds of beef and a gallon of beer. In 31 miles there were 135 bridges. This section of disused line was acquired by the National Park Authority for public access. Part of the way has been made available for wheelchairs.
⑤ The platform serviced a bobbin mill until 1961. An interpretative panel at the trackside tells its story. This is the access point for wheelchairs.

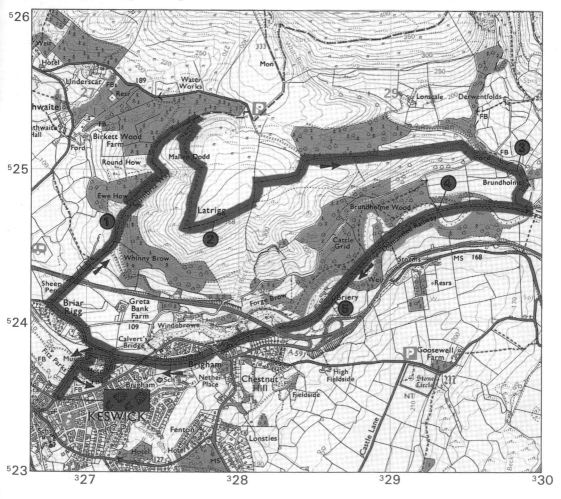

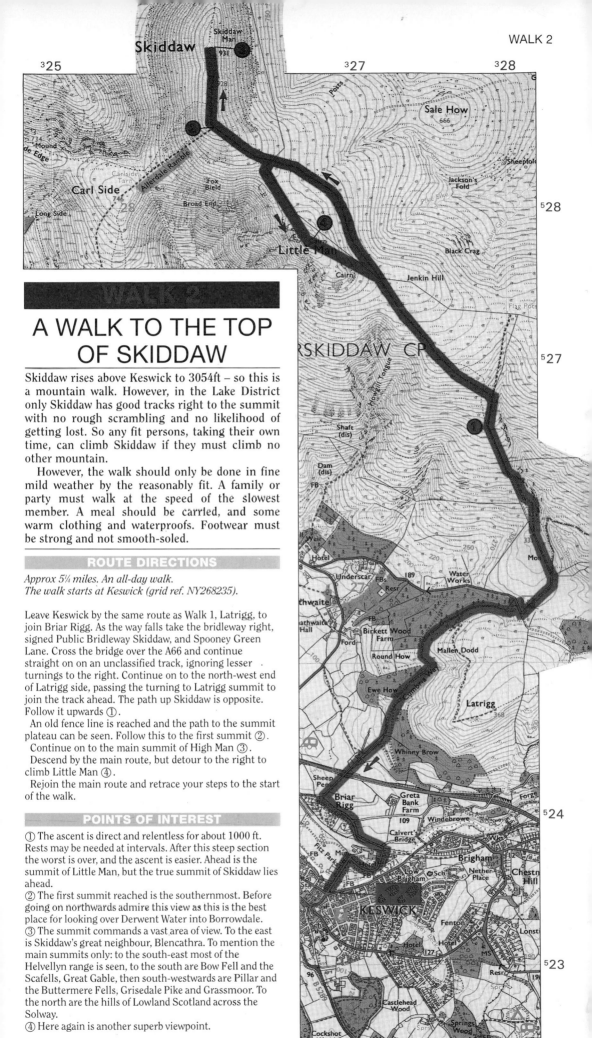

A WALK TO THE TOP OF SKIDDAW

Skiddaw rises above Keswick to 3054ft – so this is a mountain walk. However, in the Lake District only Skiddaw has good tracks right to the summit with no rough scrambling and no likelihood of getting lost. So any fit persons, taking their own time, can climb Skiddaw if they must climb no other mountain.

However, the walk should only be done in fine mild weather by the reasonably fit. A family or party must walk at the speed of the slowest member. A meal should be carried, and some warm clothing and waterproofs. Footwear must be strong and not smooth-soled.

ROUTE DIRECTIONS

Approx 5¼ miles. An all-day walk.
The walk starts at Keswick (grid ref. NY268235).

Leave Keswick by the same route as Walk 1, Latrigg, to join Briar Rigg. As the way falls take the bridleway right, signed Public Bridleway Skiddaw, and Spooney Green Lane. Cross the bridge over the A66 and continue straight on on an unclassified track, ignoring lesser turnings to the right. Continue on to the north-west end of Latrigg side, passing the turning to Latrigg summit to join the track ahead. The path up Skiddaw is opposite. Follow it upwards ①.
  An old fence line is reached and the path to the summit plateau can be seen. Follow this to the first summit ②.
  Continue on to the main summit of High Man ③.
  Descend by the main route, but detour to the right to climb Little Man ④.
  Rejoin the main route and retrace your steps to the start of the walk.

POINTS OF INTEREST

① The ascent is direct and relentless for about 1000 ft. Rests may be needed at intervals. After this steep section the worst is over, and the ascent is easier. Ahead is the summit of Little Man, but the true summit of Skiddaw lies ahead.
② The first summit reached is the southernmost. Before going on northwards admire this view as this is the best place for looking over Derwent Water into Borrowdale.
③ The summit commands a vast area of view. To the east is Skiddaw's great neighbour, Blencathra. To mention the main summits only: to the south-east most of the Helvellyn range is seen, to the south are Bow Fell and the Scafells, Great Gable, then south-westwards are Pillar and the Buttermere Fells, Grisedale Pike and Grassmoor. To the north are the hills of Lowland Scotland across the Solway.
④ Here again is another superb viewpoint.

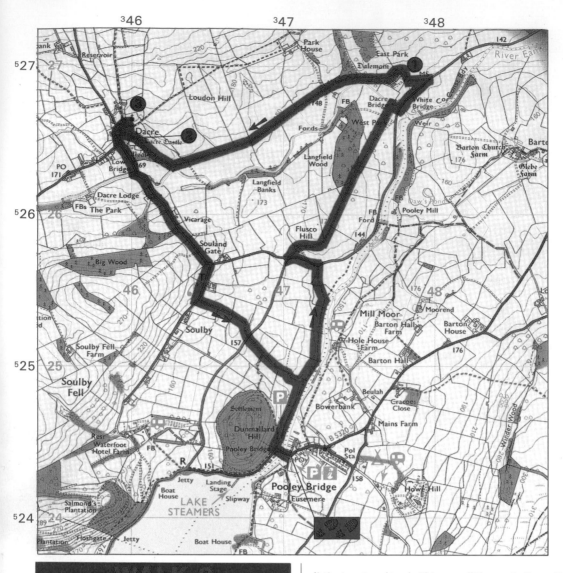

WALK 3

DALEMAIN AND DACRE

This walk goes by a historic stately home, past a medieval castle, to a church which stands on the site of an ancient monastery.

ROUTE DIRECTIONS

Approx 5½ miles. Allow 2½ – 3 hours and an extra hour or more if a visit is made to Dalemain house (see page 63) Park at one of the car parks at Pooley Bridge at the outflow of Ullswater (grid ref. NY470244).

From the west side of the bridge follow the River Eaumont by the riverside footpath. Eventually, at a kissing gate, the path takes a left turn away from the river and at a gate and stile it goes right, by the side of a double fence, and over bridges and boardwalks to join the A592. Go left along the road side, and at the first road junction go over a stone stile on the right, signed public footpath. Incline right to stile over fence and join a track which goes parallel with the road. The track goes through a series of stiles and gates with a fence on the left. It is joined by a track from the left. Eventually this leads into a field. Ahead can be seen a stone bridge. Walk towards it, but on reaching it go right, to join the road at a stile. Walk along the road side to the entrance drive to Dalemain. Walk up the drive ①.

Leave Dalemain from the yard. The right of way goes through an archway, then right between walls on a distinct westward track. This goes all the way to Dacre. At the Dacre end the way is confronted by 14th-century Dacre Castle (the castle is not normally open to the public) ②.

Walk past the castle and then take the path right to the church ③.

From the church go on to the road and go left. Ignore the first turning. Take the second turning right, signed Soulby. Just past the farm, and on a bend, a bridleway (sign) leaves left. The path is not very clear but follow the fence which is on the right. Come to the main road. Cross the road and continue in the same direction on a bridleway which leads down to the river where the walk started.

POINTS OF INTEREST

① Dalemain's Georgian front is built of a slightly purple limestone. The house has been in the family of the Hasells for over three centuries. If the house is open a visit is strongly recommended, as much for its homely atmosphere as its history. The earliest part of the building is medieval, and like all old buildings in this region, it began as a defensive tower against border raiders and then grew as the owners prospered and times became more settled.
② The castle was lost to the Dacre family when Leonard Dacre led an ill-fated revolt against Elizabeth I.
③ Excavations have proved that the church stands on the site of an Anglian monastery mentioned by the Venerable Bede. Here was signed the 'Peace of Dacre', a pact of 926 between Athelstan of England and Constantine of Scotland. In the later turbulent history of the borders the monastery was destroyed. Inside the church there are some cross shafts from the 9th century.

WALK 4

THE DERWENT WATER SHORE

Derwent Water has the advantage of a launch service from Keswick working to a timetable and circling the lake in both directions. This gives easy access for walking to half the west shore and the lake head.

Approx 3¼ miles. Allow 3 hours, including outward and return launch trips.

The walk starts with a launch trip from Keswick boat landings (grid ref. NY264227). Take the anti-clockwise service.

Disembark at Hawes End. Go south along the lake shore ①.

The path eventually leaves the lake shore for a short stretch to avoid a swamp, then rejoins it ②.

Keep to lakeshore path on to Brandelhow ③.

The path leaves the shore at Brandelhow Bay, and meets the shore again at Manesty Park ④.

The path takes a sweep round a wet area, returns, and then later goes along walkways and bridges ⑤.

Join the road and in 200yds go left, to the landing stage, after the Lodore Swiss Hotel to catch the boat back to Keswick.

① The nearest island is St Herbert's. Tradition has it that here was the 7th-century hermitage of the saint who was friend and disciple of St Cuthbert of Lindisfarne. Both saints are said to have died on the same day, in answer to a prayer of St Herbert's, in AD685. Friar's Crag, at Keswick's shore, was where visiting friars embarked to visit the hermitage to receive the saint's blessing.

② Derwent Water is a shallow lake largely due to the vast amounts of silt washed into it over many centuries by seasonal floods. It means that it is the first of the large lakes to freeze in winter. The deepest part is almost opposite and two-thirds of the way across, at 72ft. The waters contain trout, perch and pike.

③ Soon the old waste heaps of a mine are reached at Brandelhow. Vegetation and trees cover all, but the unnatural contours show that it is man-made. Just above here was a profitable lead and silver mine which was worked for centuries.

④ This land was one of the National Trust's earliest acquisitions.

⑤ From the walkways is a view of some of Borrowdale crags including Shepherd's, one of the country's most popular rock climbing crags.

WALK 5

AIRY VIEWS FROM WALLA CRAG

Although this walk involves a fairly steep ascent it is within the capabilities of any able-bodied person provided this route is followed. The less agile will take a little longer to complete it. Given a fine day the rewards are pure gold. The airy views over Derwent Water and Bassenthwaite Lake from Walla Crag are superb.

ROUTE DIRECTIONS

Approx 4¼ miles. Allow 3½ hours.
Start from Great Wood Car Park (grid ref. NY271212) on the east of the Borrowdale road, just over a mile from Keswick.

At the back of the car park at its farther end, a footpath starts left by a gate, for Ashness. Follow this path up and then right along the hillside ①.

The footpath finishes after about 1 mile at a minor road. Go left for a short distance and walk a little way above the bridge ②.

Now go back to the path and, after crossing the stile, bear right and go up the hillside. Follow the path upwards until eventually a summit cairn is reached ③.

The path continues on by a fence with steep places, and eventually meets a track and a metalled road at Rakefoot Farm. In 200yds cross the footbridge seen on the left, then bear right. Soon the path goes sharp left into Great Wood ④.

Follow the path straight down to the car park.

POINTS OF INTEREST

① The views over Derwent Water on the right are splendid.
② A classic view with the bridge in the foreground and lakes and hills behind.
③ The view is superb. Derwent Water is far below. To the south-west (left) can be seen Bow Fell, then Scafell Pike, Scafell, and Great Gable. Opposite is Catbells and behind is Eel Crag and Grisedale Pike. Northwards are Skiddaw and Blencathra, and to the south-east is the Helvellyn range. Down the crags to the left is the oddly named Lady's Rake. The story is that the Earl of Derwentwater supported the Jacobite rising of 1715 and, in spite of influence in high places, was beheaded. His young wife avoided capture when she fled Lord's Island, by climbing the crag by this 'rake' (a gully).
④ Especially lovely in springtime, Great Wood is rich in wildlife. Red and roe deer inhabit the wood, and there is a chance of seeing a red squirrel.

▼ A view of Derwent Water from below Falcon Crag

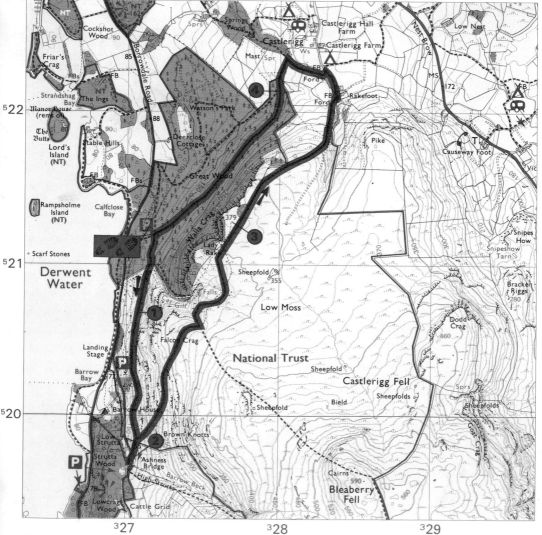

LODORE FALLS, ASHNESS

This is a walk which offers breathtaking views, away-from-it-all woodland, lakeshore, and a waterfall which was a must on the Victorian tourists' itinerary.

ROUTE DIRECTIONS

Approx 3 miles. Allow 2¾ hours.
Ideally the walk should start at the National Trust's car park on the east shore of Derwent Water (grid ref. NY267195). However, at busy holiday periods between April and October car parking is extremely limited, in which case it would be worth considering parking in Keswick, catching the service boat from Keswick landing down Derwent Water to the Lodore landing and starting the walk there.

Starting from the car park, cross the road and go left for a short distance, then go on to the footpath going right behind the wall in woodland. This follows the road side through two gates until just opposite Mary Mount where it goes into the wood and reaches the north bank of Lodore waterfalls.

Starting from the Lodore landing, go beyond and behind the Lodore Hotel, then over a footbridge to reach the same spot ①.

The route goes upwards to a point above the falls. A path can be seen which appears to offer a route entirely in the wrong direction – going upwards into the woodland on the left. This, however, is the way. Follow it, keeping right at a fork, and in a few minutes a path will be seen leaving it in a sharp zig-zag right, back towards the beck. The path then goes up rocky steps parallel with the beck. At a fork above the falls, keep left on the path which continues climbing. This becomes a terraced path and continues through the woodland. At a Y-junction follow the main path, climbing gradually right. The path zig-zags first away from the sound of the beck, then goes parallel with it. At a T-junction with a main track, go left to reach a tarmac, unclassified road. Follow the road side and in a little while there is a small car park right, and opposite is a viewpoint ②.

Now follow the road side down, and just past another small car park in woodland there is a humped-back bridge over Barrow Beck, Ashness Bridge ③.

Follow the road side down the hill to the Borrowdale road. Turn left on it for a short distance and opposite the Youth Hostel gate go over a stile leading on to a peninsula. Follow the path going right around it to a footbridge ④.

The path continues to join a roadside causeway leading to the car park start. If, alternatively, the walk started at Lodore, take the route from this car park as detailed at the beginning of the Route Directions, going back behind the Lodore Hotel.

POINTS OF INTEREST

① At Lodore Falls Watendlath Beck drops 120 feet before its journey's end into the lake. The sight might be a disappointment if there has been dry weather, but at other times it can be quite thrilling.
② This is Surprise View. From this point, perched high on a sheer cliff above Lodore Wood, framed by trees, is a stupendous prospect over the whole of Derwent Water. To the north is Keswick, with Skiddaw and Bassenthwaite Lake beyond.
③ Walk up the beck and look towards the little bridge with the view of the lake and mountains beyond and you may recognise a perfect picture which has probably been on more chocolate boxes, greetings cards, and calendars than any other view in England!
④ Here is the best view anywhere of Skiddaw, across an expanse of lake.

A STROLL AROUND BUTTERMERE

The lakes of Crummock Water and Buttermere – both under National Trust protection – share a valley amid some of the Lake District's wildest and grandest scenery. Buttermere village is the starting point for this delightful walk round Windermere's shores. It is a walk to savour, and with a picnic meal could last most of the day.

ROUTE DIRECTIONS

Approx 4¼ miles. Allow 2 hours.
Start at Buttermere village (grid ref. NY175170).

Follow the track starting to the left of the Fish Hotel and keep left, ignoring a branch right that heads up towards Scale Force ①.

In ¼ mile go over bridges and keep left, following the path parallel to lake shore ②.

At the head of the lake turn left over the bridge and follow the path to Gatesgarth Farm and a metalled road. Turn left on to the road, follow it for ½ mile and then turn left again between gateposts on to the lakeshore path ③.

Continue on the path along a lakeside terrace before passing through a tunnel ④.

Follow the path beyond the end of the lake. Go through the farmyard back to the start.

POINTS OF INTEREST

① The long strands of falling water ahead form Sourmilk Gill, spilling from Bleaberry Tarn. This little mountain lake is hidden away in a combe high above, between the peaks of Red Pike and High Stile.

② Less than 1½ miles long and 90ft deep, Buttermere was probably ancient 'Buthar's Mere', Buthar being a Norse settler. The area bristles with Norse names. The mountains are 'fells' from Norse 'fjall', streams are 'becks' (bekr), ravines are 'gills', small lakes 'tarns' (tjorn), waterfalls 'forces' (foss). The Vikings settled here in large numbers in the 9th and 10th centuries, it is presumed peacefully. Some were Christians, and they came as agriculturists and sheep farmers. The clear lake is over 90ft deep and contains trout, and the deep-water fish of the trout family, 'char', a species left from the Ice Age.

③ The path goes by Shingle Point under pine trees. Left and above the head of the lake is Fleetwith Pike. To the right of that is Haystacks and the sweep of fell side called Warnscale (Norse 'Skali', summer pasture) and the peaks of High Crag, High Stile, and Red Pike. The two great hollows, or 'combes', were scooped out by retreating ice in the Ice Age.

④ The tunnel is cut through a wall of solid rock. Story has it that the one-time landowner hated to see his gardeners idle on wet days, and so he put them to the task of tunnelling to keep them occupied. The path emerges to meander through lakeside trees.

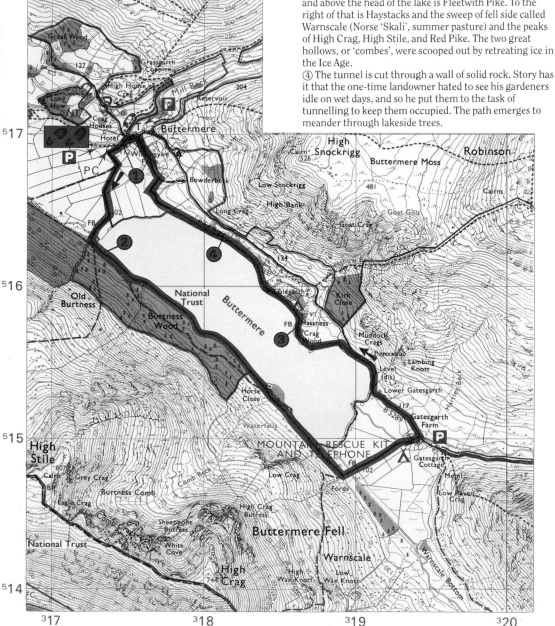

WALK 8

KELDAS, LANTY'S TARN AND GRISEDALE VALLEY

After a short steep start on this walk there are tremendous views over Ullswater, then after passing a small tarn the walk explores the Grisedale valley, returning by the old pack-horse route linking Grasmere and Patterdale.

ROUTE DIRECTIONS

Approx 6 miles. Allow 3½ hours.
Park in the public car park at Glenridding (grid ref. NY386169).

From the car park walk back to the main road, turn right to cross the bridge, then right again to follow the track alongside Glenridding Beck. At a fork in the track keep left, signed Lanty Tarn, Helvellyn. Follow the track to the end and then go left over a little footbridge. Time needs to be taken over the steep but short ascent which is now faced – this is the hardest part of the whole walk. After a kissing gate follow the path right, and then at a wall and another gate go left, signposted Striding Edge and Grisedale.

A kissing gate is reached and Lanty's Tarn can be seen beyond; but delay going this way. Turn left before the gate and go through the wall gap and on to the pine-clad hill, using any of the paths ①.

Return down to the kissing gate and walk on past Lanty's Tarn and down the track. It turns right and levels off and there is a gate and kissing gate. Go through this and there is a fork with the clearer path going right; take the more level way left, signed (in wall) Grasmere, Grisedale Tarn, and continue on ②.

Eventually the pass summit can be seen ahead. At the end of a plantation the path descends through a series of hillocks ③.

The path crosses a footbridge and after this, before the path reaches a wall, there is a sheep-fold. Go left here just before it to follow a faint green path down to a gate and footbridge. After crossing the bridge bear left to join a very clear track. Go left with it ④.

Follow this track and road all the way down to the road at Glenridding. When the pavement peters out at the end of Patterdale Hall land, a footpath can be followed along the woodland fringe left. This ends at the boat landings, where you can cross the road and finish the walk at the picnic area.

POINTS OF INTEREST

① Here are superb views of Ullswater, framed in pines – a photographer's dream.
② Grisedale is old Norse for 'valley of pigs'. As you continue on this path there is a view of the heights at the head of Grisedale which belong to the southern end of the Helvellyn range. Dollywaggon Pike (2810ft) is on the left, and Nethermost Pike right. On the left of the gap is Fairfield (2863ft).
③ The mounds are moraine heaps – piles of debris left by the retreating ice, most probably at the end of the last 'mini' Ice Age, around 9000BC.
④ This is the old pack-horse track. The peculiar-shaped ash trees are a result of pollarding in times past. The trees were cut at above cattle height and the branches thrown down for fodder.

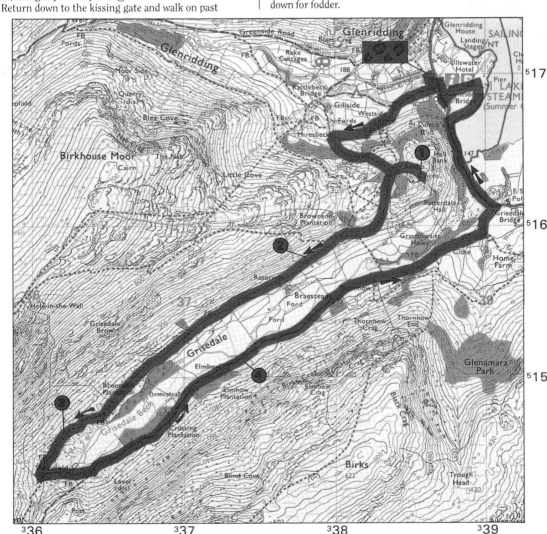

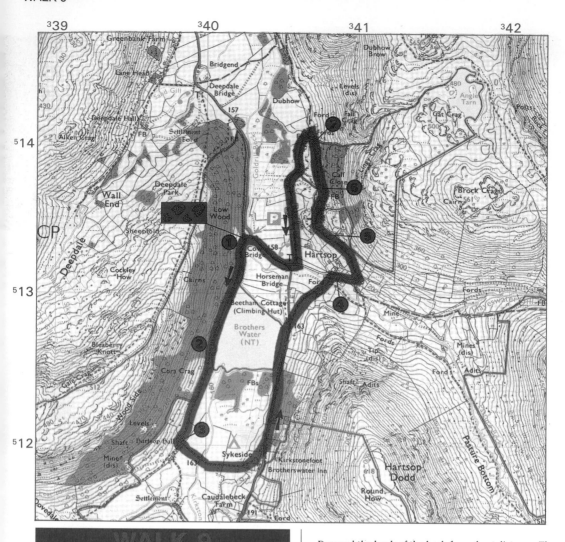

WALK 9

BROTHERS WATER AND HARTSOP

This walk goes along the banks of Brothers Water at the northern foot of Kirkstone Pass, through the old unspoilt hamlet of Hartsop, and below the wooded crags of Calf Close.

ROUTE DIRECTIONS

Approx 3½ miles. Allow 2¾ hours.
Park at Cow Bridge (grid ref. NY403134).

Go across the bridge, through the gate and on to the track on the west bank of Brothers Water ①.
  Walk along the lakeside track ②.
  Beyond the head of the lake the track continues to Hartsop Hall farm ③.
  Turn left immediately after the farm, left again and then through a gate on to a track. Just before reaching the Brothers Water Inn, take the roadway left. Before this reaches the Kirkstone road there is a gate left on to a footpath. Follow this. The way goes by the east shore of Brothers Water.
  The path rises from the shore to a kissing gate. Go through this and directly across the road to join a green footpath between walls. This goes by cottages to a footbridge. Cross this and go right, through the village ④.
  Walk on through the village almost to the end of the macadam road past a fork, and then go left on a steep track through a gate. Continue on ⑤.
  The track divides three ways. Continue straight ahead. The track narrows to a footpath under wooded crags ⑥.
  The path finishes at a stile. Cross this ⑦.

Descend the bank of the beck for a short distance. Then there is a choice. If the water is low enough, ford the beck, descend on the far side, and cross the footbridge. Otherwise, one can continue to make an undignified scramble down the bank. There is a farm gate left. Go through this and along the track between walls. Follow this to the end. Go right to the main road, and right again to the car park.

POINTS OF INTEREST

① It was on the bridge on a spring day that William Wordsworth in a happy mood wrote the poem *Written in March While Resting on the Bridge at the Foot of Brothers' Water*. It begins:
      The Cock is crowing,
      The stream is flowing,
      The small birds twitter,
      The lake doth glitter.
② Before the late 18th century, Brothers Water was shown on maps as 'Broad Water'. Wordsworth ascribes the change of name to a tragic accident that is said to have happened on a New Year's Day after that time. The lake had frozen, and two local brothers were out sliding on the ice when it gave way and both were drowned.
③ The old part of the building dates from the 16th century.
④ Here are some 17th-century cottages, some with so-called spinning galleries. In fact, in earlier times many of the cottagers' tasks would be done here, in shelter and in better light than could be obtained indoors.
⑤ There are some excellent views over Brothers Water from the track's summit. To the left of Hartsop Hall rises High Hartsop Dod. On the Dod's right is the valley of Dovedale. Dove Crag (2603ft), on the Fairfield range, stands behind.
⑥ This is a delightfully wild area.
⑦ This is Angletarn Beck waterfall – a place to linger.

WALK 10

WORDSWORTH'S FOOTSTEPS

The walk around Grasmere should be obligatory for all who wish to savour the true essence of Wordsworth's Lake District. It could be combined with a visit to Dove Cottage, Wordsworth's home, and the museum.

ROUTE DIRECTIONS

Approx 4 miles. Allow 2 hours (longer if a visit to Dove Cottage is included)
The walk starts at Grasmere village (grid ref. NY336065).

Take the minor road south-west for Langdale. After climbing for a mile, pass the Hunting Stile junction then watch for and go left down a path to the lake shore ①.
  The walk rounds the end of the lake past a weir. Cross the footbridge into the wood opposite, then bear right to walk on above the river side to emerge on to a field and then on to White Moss Common. Walk upwards to the left and cross the main road with care. A little way to the left, opposite, is a minor road climbing upwards. Take this. In ¼ mile, at the top of the hill, leave the road and go right on a footpath to a viewpoint on a rocky knoll ②.
  Go back to the road and continue on ③.
  At the junction go left, and descend to Dove Cottage ④.
  Cross the road with care and walk back into Grasmere village. Go into St Oswald's churchyard, and turn right to the Wordsworth graves ⑤.

POINTS OF INTEREST

① Rowing boats can be hired at various points round Grasmere.
② The view to the south-east over Rydal Water is one to linger at.

▲ Dove Cottage, home to the poet William Wordsworth

③ The wood on the right was John Wordsworth's favourite place to visit when he stayed with his brother William. John was a ship's captain, who was tragically drowned at sea – the wood subsequently became known as 'John's Wood'.
④ Dove Cottage, by the foot of the hill is open to the public. Here William and his sister Dorothy settled in 1799. Later William married and brought his bride Mary here. The house became too small for a growing family and they left in 1808. However, during his time at Dove Cottage the poet wrote some of his greatest works, including *Intimations of Immortality, The Prelude* and many shorter works. Next to Dove Cottage is an excellent museum and gallery. This, and the extensive library of documents and manuscripts, brings thousands of students of English literature here from all over the world. Mention must also be made of the author Thomas de Quincey, who married a local girl and took the tenancy of Dove Cottage after the Wordsworths left.
⑤ Wordsworth chose a modest resting place. His wife Mary is buried with him. Dora, their daughter, is in the next grave.

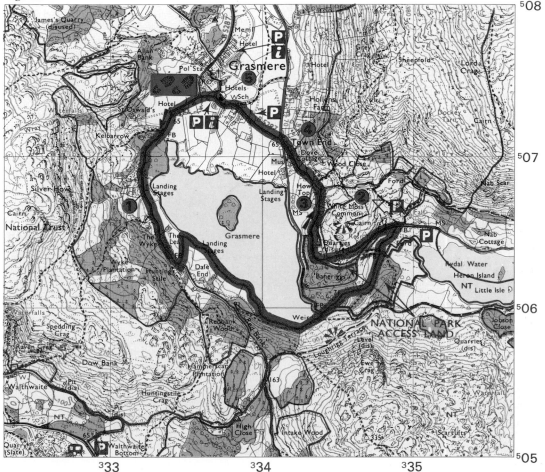

SWEDEN BRIDGE

An away-from-it-all from Ambleside up tracks overhung by trees, with wide views, picturesque old arched bridges and cascading waterfalls. A steady ascent and descent of 550ft. Not for anyone in a hurry.

ROUTE DIRECTIONS

Approx 3 miles. Allow 2½ hours.
Start the walk at Ambleside market cross (grid ref. NY377046).

Go up North Road to Kirkstone Road and after about 200yds turn left down Sweden Bridge Lane. At the next junction bear right. At the following junction go on by Sweden Bridge Lane for High Sweden Bridge ①.
 In 1¼ miles cross High Sweden Bridge ②.
 Immediately after crossing the stream go left and then right, following an ascending path to the left of a wall. Cross the stile at the top of the rise and bear left to follow the path to a stone-walled sheep-fold. Go right round a sheep-pen, over a stile on the left and descend the track (keeping dogs on leads) ③.
 In ¾ mile cross Low Sweden Bridge ④.
 Follow the lane down into Ambleside.

POINTS OF INTEREST

① This was once a busy pack-pony and cart track from Ambleside to Hartsop and Patterdale. In the stone walls to the right of the path is Mountain Parsley fern, an alpine common in the Lake District and very choosy in its habitat. The wayside trees include thickets of blackthorn (sloe), hazel, rowan, and hawthorn trees. Flowers include foxglove, meadowsweet in the wetter areas, and in 'heath' type banks the harebell and the tiny yellow four-petalled flower, the tormentil (once a herb used to cure 'the torments').
② This is a beautiful old arched bridge. Notice the water-worn rocks below.
③ Here from the sheep pasture is a view over Ambleside and the upper part of the lake.
④ This is a larger but also beautiful bridge with fine waterfalls.

▼ Seventeenth-century Bridge House, perched over Stock Ghyll in Ambleside

THE WAST WATER SCREES

Much has been made by writers of the fierce drama of Wasdale; 'horrifying', 'over-powering', is how some have described it. Indeed the view from the Gosforth road of the great mass of Wasdale Screes, 1700ft high and apparently sliding loose into the deepest lake in England, is certainly dramatic. But Wast Water also holds its delights, and one of them is a classic view from the lake foot. This walk takes in the delight and the drama.

ROUTE DIRECTIONS

Approx 5¼ miles. Allow 2¼ hours.
The walk starts at Nether Wasdale (grid ref. SD126040)
①.

Walk eastwards for ¼ mile along the road to the junction, go right and over the bridge, then immediately left on the track to Easthwaite Farm. Go left at the farm buildings. In ¼ mile at a junction in the path bear left to cross the bridge, then turn right to follow the path to the lake shore ②.

Go along the shore and in front of Wasdale Hall (Youth Hostel) ③.

Continue on and emerge on to a road and go right along the road side for about ½ mile to the junction ④.

Turn left and follow the road side, and in ½ mile cross the bridge at Greendale, then turn left on to a signposted footpath. Follow the path straight through until it goes between walls and emerges after 1¼ miles on to a minor road. Turn right to return to the starting point.

The Wasdale screes, nothing if not dramatic ▶

POINTS OF INTEREST

① Formerly known as strands, Nether Wasdale is the gateway to the remote awe-inspiring valley that shelters Wast Water.
② This is National Trust land, and soon the view up the lake, framed in trees, is before you. Behind the lake are the humps of Yewbarrow, Kirkfell and Great Gable, with Lingmell, a spur of Scafell, on the right.
③ The hall was built in 1826. In its early occupancy the child of the house was accidentally drowned in the lake and the area is said to be haunted by the mother and child. The hall is now a Youth Hostel.
④ The remarkable Wast Water Screes are immediately opposite the lakeside road just here. The fell was undercut by the slowly moving glacier that scooped out the 258ft-deep lake at the end of the Ice Age, and it has remained at its present unstable angle for 12,000 years. Sometimes a huge mass thunders down. But local people can point out some massive boulders which have been poised seemingly precariously as far back as can be remembered. The water is very clear indeed and because it is not rich in nutrients supports little animal and plant life.

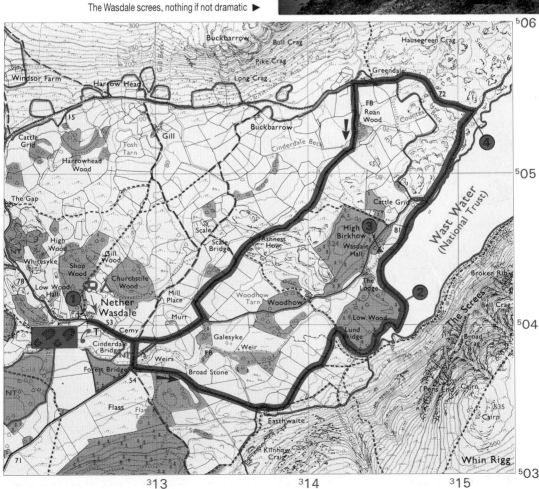

LOUGHRIGG TARN AND ELTERWATER

On offer here is a waterfall, and classic viewpoints over a lovely tarn and across one of the Lake District's smallest and most charming lakes. As part of the walk is on low-lying fields, it could be a 'wellies' walk after periods of rain.

ROUTE DIRECTIONS

Approx 3½ miles. Allow 2½ hours.
Park in Silverthwaite Car Park (NT), a short distance north-west from Skelwith Bridge on the Langdale road, on the right (grid ref. NY341037).

On the opposite side of the road from the car park there is a gap in the low wall. A footpath descends through woodland from here to a field below. On reaching the field go left and head for a riverside gate. Beyond is a clear track. Follow this. The track soon reaches Skelwith Force waterfall ①.

Continue on the riverside track and through the yards of the Kirkstone Greenslate Quarries Company ②.

Continue on to join the road at the bridge. Go left past the Skelwith Bridge Hotel. At the road junction just past here, a minor road can be seen ascending steeply, directly opposite. Walk up this. When this road reaches a T-junction go right for a short distance, then go left on a macadam lane. Go right in front of the cottages on a track. At track junction go immediately left through a gate and along the track beyond. The Tarn is soon reached ③.

Continue on to the lane-end gate. Join the road and go left. At the first junction go right down the minor road, and at the next junction go straight ahead. At the junction with the Langdale road go right. After the gate and cattle grid Elterwater Common is reached. Walk along the road side and take the first minor road on the left into Elterwater village ④.

Walk to the bridge over the beck. Just before it a permissive footpath goes from a gate in the little car park along the beck side. Follow this. The path leaves the beck side through woodland and eventually, at a gate, touches the eastern extremity of Elterwater ⑤.

The path now crosses fields (possibly wet) parallel to what is now the River Brathay. The stile to the path from which the walk started is up on the left at the far end of a small wood.

POINTS OF INTEREST

① Bridges lead to viewpoints. Although the fall is not high, it can often be spectacular as the volume of water is considerable, taking the flows from all the high fells facing Great and Little Langdale.
② In the sheds here the local, unusually hard slate is cut by a diamond-toothed saw, and polished. Examples of the slate's great beauty can be seen around. It is exported worldwide, often used for facing prestigious buildings. There is a gallery on the right where slate items can be seen and purchased.
③ This to William Wordsworth was:

Diana's Looking Glass – Loughrigg Tarn, round, clear and bright as heaven . . .

Across the splendid foreground of the water, there is a much pictured view of Langdale Pikes.
④ From 1824 to the first quarter of this century, Elterwater was the scene of a busy gunpowder mill powered by six water wheels.
⑤ Here there is a classic view again of Langdale Pikes over the waters of 'swan lake' ('Elter' is Norse for 'swan').

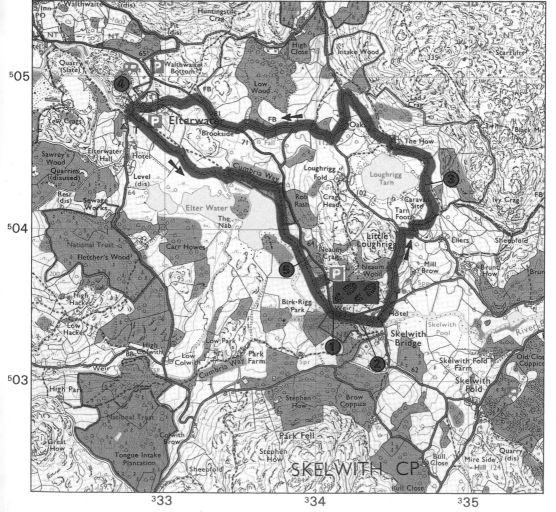

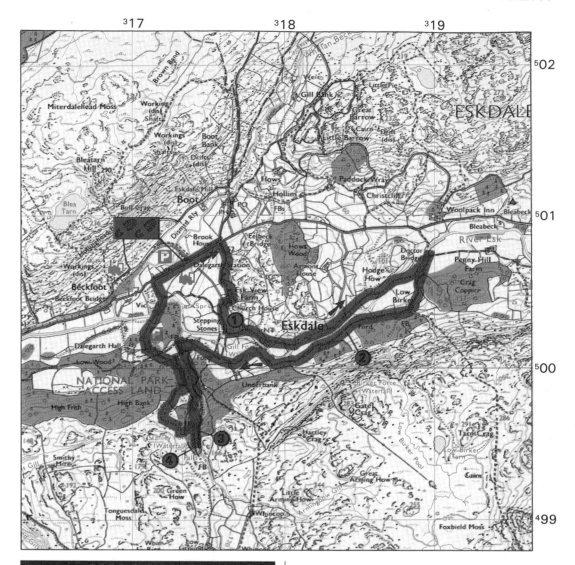

WALK 14

ESKDALE AND STANLEY FORCE WATERFALL

The River Esk rises below the Scafells and flows through the pink granite of the Eskdale valley. Along its banks are some of the best scenic walks in the Lake District. This walk includes a visit to Dalegarth, or Stanley Force waterfall, which flows dramatically through a wooded gorge.

ROUTE DIRECTIONS

Approx 4 miles. Allow 2½ hours.
Park in Dalegarth Station car park (grid ref. NY173007),
or alternatively park at Ravenglass and take the narrow-
gauge railway service to this terminal.

From the station car park join the road and go left towards Boot. At Boot go first right on a by-way for the church ①.
  From the church go to the river bank, turn left signed Public Footpath Doctor Bridge, go through a kissing gate and on. The path rises above the river and goes between walls and on a terrace to Doctor Bridge. Cross the bridge, then go right again, signed Dalegarth. The way goes by Low Birker, and along a track between walls. The way levels out. Cross a footbridge. The track is plain to see, sometimes stony, sometimes green ②.
  Cross a little ford by stepping stones just before a track

doubles back for the church, which should be ignored. Continue on and follow the track through a gate into wooded National Park access land, and cross a footbridge. Follow the way to a gate, but do not go through it. Turn left by the wall side and join a plain path which goes on through the wood by the beck. Two bridges are crossed and then there is a viewpoint bridge ③.
  There is no further access here. Double back and take the path which ascends on steps to the left, steeply at first, following a beck. At its T-junction go left and up to a viewpoint. **Warning** – the viewpoint stands over a sheer cliff and children should be kept close ④.
  Follow the path from the viewpoint to a stile over the wall. Walk on to the track beyond and descend, following the track all the way without deviation on to a macadam roadway which joins the Eskdale road at a T-junction. Turn right for Dalegarth Station.

POINTS OF INTEREST

① This is a typical Dales church, built like a barn. Eskdale was once the preserve of the Cistercian monks of Calder and its mother abbey of Furness, and they had a chapel here. Until the beginning of this century the graveyard, as well as serving Eskdale, had to take burials from Wasdale, which had no consecrated ground. Funeral processions had to negotiate the wild moorland tracks to the west. Note the well-sculpted gravestone of Tommy Dobson, local huntsman.
② This is a very pleasant, away-from-it-all scene. A little tarn is passed. The redness underfoot betrays the presence of iron. One of Eskdale's mine levels was off the track left.
③ The bridge offers a view of the lower part of the falls.
④ There is a great prospect here over Eskdale to the high fells.

WALK 15

CONISTON LAKE SHORE

The walk along Coniston Water's shore offers scores of delightful viewpoints and picnic spots. Its return over the heights of Torver Back Common gives a rare feeling of remoteness and offers wonderful panoramic views.

ROUTE DIRECTIONS

Approx 7½ miles. Allow 4¼ hours.
Park in Coniston village (grid ref. SD303976).

From Coniston village walk south over the bridge, and take the turning left down the road which leads to the boat landings. At the sharp bend in the road cross the stile on to a footpath signed Coniston Hall. The path eventually joins another plain track, going left and then right for Coniston Hall ①.

Continue on the surfaced track after the Hall, past the yacht club trailer park and into the campsite. Go left to the lake shore. Follow the shore-line on ②.

The path continues for over two miles.

Eventually the path leaves the shore by the side of a wall, bears right away from it, goes through a gate and joins the Torver road. Go right and walk alongside the road on the right-hand bank until opposite the garage, where there is a path going right, by the wall. This goes through a gate on to the access land, and passes Kelly Tarn. A path goes on by a wall to reach another tarn, Long Moss. Take the path rising to the viewpoint hill to its right ③.

Follow the path on. After crossing a beck there is a boggy area and the path is obscure. The way is on a rising green path with a craggy knoll on its right. Eventually the way leads to a path going down by a beck side through junipers and woodland towards the lake. At the shore-line path, go left for Coniston Hall. After the Hall follow the track and the footpath which can be clearly seen heading for the road back into Coniston village.

POINTS OF INTEREST

① The hall (NT) with its massive round chimneys, which are typical of the oldest buildings in the Lake District, dates from 16th century, and was the home of the Le Flemings who made their fortune from the local mines.

② Traces of slag may be found in the lakeshore pebbles, all that is left of small 'bloomeries' where iron was smelted crudely, using charcoal from the surrounding woodland. The ore was brought to the shore line by boat.

③ There are airy views here over the lake. Five miles long and 180ft deep at its deepest point, this is the lake where Donald Campbell was killed while attempting to break the world water speed record in 1967 in his boat *Bluebird*.

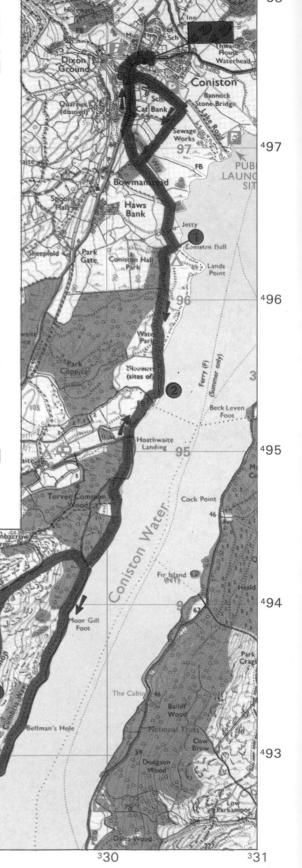

THE HEIGHTS OF CLAIFE

This is a varied walk from Bowness-on-Windermere along lakeshore lanes, rough tracks, hill and woodland paths.

ROUTE DIRECTIONS

Approx 8 miles. Allow 4½ hours.
Start from Bowness Pier (grid ref. SD401968).

Walk south-west past the information centre and the shoreside business premises. At the far end an iron gate leads on to a footpath which goes round the lake shore and joins the road to the ferry. Cross on the ferry ①.

Disembark and walk by the buildings of Ferry House to pick up a footpath going right, by the lakeside side of some fish tanks. This joins a lakeside road. Turn right on to this road. The metalled road finishes and becomes a track through woodland ②.

The track leaves the shore as it goes round Strawberry Gardens, but continues on the other side. A shore path goes parallel with the track if preferred. After 1 mile the wall of Belle Grange is reached ③.

This is the rough track to be taken. In under ¼ mile, near the top of the hill, a path is seen joining from the left across a stream. Take this route. This climbs for a while then levels out on to a terrace walk ④.

The path comes to some rocky knolls and to a T-junction. Descend here on a path which leaves the wood to follow a woodland boundary on its left. After some wet sections the track is joined by another from the right. Continue for a further ¼ mile to a T-junction, and go left. Continue without deviation. The path dives down through a wood. After ⅓ mile watch for and take a path turning sharp right down to the shore road hiding behind buildings below. Descend and in ¼ mile join the shore road, cross by the ferry, turn left by the car park and continue by footpath and minor road past the cemetery to the pier and the starting point.

POINTS OF INTEREST

① The first mention of a ferry at Bowness was in 1454.
② There are fine trees of all kinds but look for the massive trunks of sweet chestnut, and tall columns of Douglas Fir.
③ This rough ascending track was once used by carts and coaches! There was an old ferry route to Belle Grange from Millerground on the far side of the lake.
④ There is a hidden quarry by this path called 'Crier of Claife', for it was here in the 18th century that a fearsome ghost which terrorised the area with its chilling screams was finally put to rest by an exorcising priest.

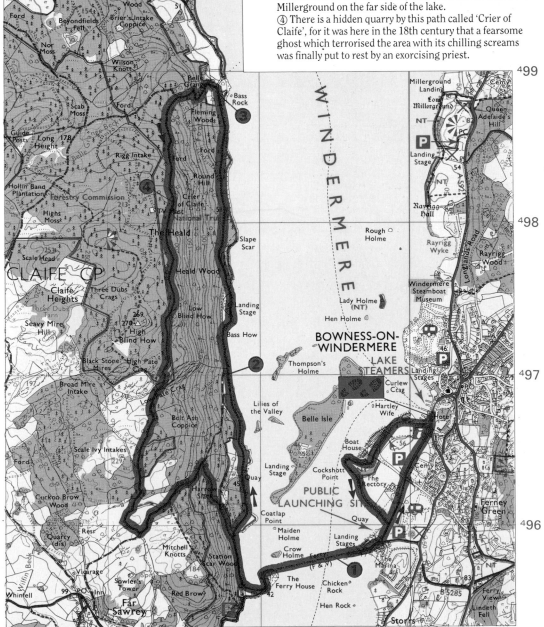

ACKNOWLEDGEMENTS

The Automobile Association wishes to thank the following photographers, libraries and associations for their assistance in the preparation of this book.

Abbot Hall Museum of Lakeland Life & Industry, Kendal 17 Swallows & Amazons; *Heather Angel* 10/1 Red deer, 13 Yellow Flag; *Ardea London* 12 Golden Eagle, Purple Saxifrage, Buzzard; *E A Bowness* 18 Climber, 19 Walkers, 20/1 Runner, 20 Foxhounds, 21 Wrestling, Hound Trailing, Fell Runners; *J Bowness* 44 Mountain Rescue Exercise; *Cumbria Tourist Board* 15 Dove Cottage, 43 Lakeland Fare; *Fotobank* 14/5 Daffodils; *Freshwater Biological Society* 13 Vendace, Char; *Mary Evans Picture Library* 61 Hawes Water; *EDMUND NAGELE* Cover Derwent Water; *The Mansell Collection* 14 William Wordsworth, Mary Wordsworth, 16 Coleridge, Southey

All remaining pictures are held in the Association's own picture library (A A Photo Library) with contributions from: E A Bowness, R Czaja, S King, P Sharpe, R Surman

Other Ordnance Survey Maps of the Lake District

How to get there with the Routemaster and Tourist Series

Reach the Lake District from Manchester, Leeds or Carlisle and other parts of Northern England with Sheet 5 Northern England of the Routemaster Series.
Access from Penrith, Kendal, Cockermouth or Broughton-in-Furness is shown on the Lake District Tourist Map.

Exploring with the Landranger and Outdoor Leisure Maps

Landranger Series
1¼ inches to one mile or 1 : 50 000 scale
These maps cover the whole of Britain and are good for local motoring and walking. Each contains tourist information such as parking, picnic places, viewpoints and rights of way. Sheets covering the Lake District are:
89 West Cumbria
90 Penrith and Keswick
96 South Lakeland
97 Kendal and Morecambe

Outdoor Leisure Series
2½ inches to one mile or 1 : 25 000 scale
These maps for walkers show the countryside of Britain in great detail, including field boundaries and rights of way in England and Wales.
The maps with the walks in this book are extracted from the Outdoor Leisure Maps of the Lake District. There are four sheets in the series:
The English Lakes NW Sheet
The English Lakes NE Sheet
The English Lakes SW Sheet
The English Lakes SE Sheet

Other titles available in this series are:
Brecon Beacons; Channel Islands; Cornwall; Cotswolds; Days out from London; Devon and Exmoor; East Anglia; Forest of Dean and Wye Valley; Ireland; Isle of Wight; New Forest; Northumbria; North York Moors; Peak District; Scottish Highlands; Snowdonia; South Downs; Wessex; Yorkshire Dales